mother country
by peggy leon

the permanent press
sag harbor, ny 11963

Copyright© 2003 by Peggy Leon

Library of Congress Cataloging-in-Publication Data

Leon, Peggy
      Mother Country / by Peg Leon
        p. cm.
      ISBN 1-57962-095-7
      I. Title.

      PS3612.E368 M68 2003
      813'.6--dc22

                    2003017033

Printed in The United States of America

THE PERMANENT PRESS
4170 Noyac Road
Sag Harbor, NY 11963

For John and Diana....

After Words

I live in a green place now, a place of streams and ponds and tree-shrouded hills, of mists and rain and heavy snow. It is beautiful, but it's not my home. Green does not come naturally to me. I can't trust it. I am more comfortable with shades of gray, the desert emptiness where I grew up, and its ghosts.

Ghosts come in all forms.

An afternoon's northwest wind still brings me around, eyes in slits, searching for the line of restless tumbleweeds, the distant wall of dust building and advancing. It would have to travel east more than 2,500 miles from Taylor, Nevada to reach me, but I can taste its bitter first breath. I know the feel of it along my skin, at the roots of my hair. Far off thunder brings me the tangy scent of wet sagebrush. I still know the evaporating promise of rain falling from black clouds, disappearing before it wets my upturned face.

Ghosts of water, wind, and land. Ghosts of people, too.

I still hear the thickly accented voices of old people, crotchety miners, their stern-faced wives and widows. They've been dead a long time, their ways forgotten, but not by me. I carry them. They emerge from my memory whenever they choose, dusting themselves off and telling me what to do. They're as sure as they ever were that I need their advice. The women wear black: black babushkas, black misshapen sweaters buttoned over heavy breasts, black skirts, black stockings, black sturdy shoes. Wind and sun and hard work have carved their faces. Beware, my little old ladies are not the polite, tea-drinking sort. They like a shot of whiskey after dinner. They are blunt in their opinions. They learned how to swear from their husbands, who learned how to swear first and best. There is nothing little about them.

5

These women are wise, and I am glad of their company. Sometimes they squat or pace around me, a flock of crows as I work my garden. *Too many rocks,* one will comment. *This dirt need something,* another murmurs as she prods the soil with crooked fingers. *Some little chicken shit. Do like this,* her hands work the soil gently. *No, no. Too damn strong. Maybe cow shit better,* another argues. *No, no,* a third joins in, *too many weeds. Sheep best for garden.* Eventually, they are all drawn into this argument. I poke and turn the soil with my trowel, awaiting their decision.

In the kitchen, they watch me closely. Six handfuls of this, two pinches of that. Measuring cups and spoons are not required. Boxed cakes are scorned. The hand mixer is too loud; they prefer the satisfying thwap, thwap of a wooden spoon against a glass bowl. *Use whole arm,* one orders. *Maybe little more salt,* another states. At this point they are liable to argue: who makes the best bread, whose Easter cake is the lightest. When the finished product is pulled from the oven, they gather around to sample the fragrant steam. *Smell pretty damn good,* one says at last. We all nod.

The old men are not interested in my garden or my kitchen. They want to know what I'm drinking. They sniff at the bottles on the sideboard and mumble amongst themselves. They spurn the gin, are mystified by the tequila, a little suspicious of the single malt. *Twelve years, twelve days,* they snort. *No difference. All same!* Some nights, as I sit at the table having a glass of wine with dinner, Eli, my stepgrandfather, dead since I was eight, hovers near my elbow. His trousers are worn and washed to the color of slate, his sweater so thin the pattern of his plaid shirt shows through. Wine is his expertise. He is a veteran of boxcars of wine grapes shipped to our desert town, then divvied up among families. He is king of the press, arbiter of aging, a judge. Sniffing at my glass he pulls a face. *No good stuff,* he warns. *Too sour!* I remember that other wine, a stolen taste with giggling cousins, sweet, thick, basement cool, a breath of danger on my tongue, the touch of Ball jar threads against my lip. Perhaps Eli is right. Perhaps some things can be left too long on a shelf. Some things need to be tasted when they are young and sweet.

In fall here, when the green outside is smeared with rain and rising mist, I see them all gather round my picture window, shaking their heads at the dark day. *Taylor never like this,* one says. *Sun there, always sun... That hell a lot of water,* another comments. *Pretty damn green,* someone adds. *Like Old Country,* a small voice says. *Old Country,* someone snorts. *Who remember Old Country? This America!* There is silence as they watch the weeping trees. *I remember,* a tentative voice admits. Soon they are all nodding solemnly. The old women cross themselves and kiss their fingertips gently. A prayer for what has been left behind. So, as I sit on the couch, with a child tucked under each arm and a bright blanket over our laps, I remember them. They are remembering, too.

The children shake me from this reverie. *Mommy, tell us a story. Tell us about Taylor. Yes, tell us about The Sands. No, about Naked Sal. No, not that one. Tell us about Grandpa's boxing trip! No, Mommy, tell us about..."*

Old men and women turn from the window and nod. *Yes, yes, tell them, tell them. Remember us...*

Outside the mists have thickened, the garden and the hillside beyond painted opalescent shades of gray. *Shh...* I hush them all. *Shh, I'll tell you a story.*

I remember a summer full of stories, stories told and made, that I gathered and carried away. It was the summer my grandmother died; Naked Sal walked the streets of Taylor for the last time unashamed; Johnny Miniverri came out of his padded closet in the In-home Diner, stood on The Sands and heard the earth moving on its axis; old miners' widows sat in a circle in a dim front room, a convocation of crows,

7

with tea, cake and gossip, turning the Holy Wheel of our town. It was the summer of 1950, when my beautiful, invincible, cousin Josie climbed into a 1936 Buick that had never been driven out of first gear and headed out of Taylor east toward a Boston college. She was the first in our family to go. I wanted to be her mother, or her child. I was thirteen, and with the death of Gram, alone.

Part 1

1

The loneliest road in America ran straight through the middle of Taylor, Nevada. There was a sign to prove it. It stood by the side of the highway, the only thing over three feet high in an endless alkali flat scattered with cheat grass, sagebrush, jackrabbits, and rattlesnakes. *Highway 50. The loneliest road in America.* A string of dusty towns, some no more than a cottonwood and a hopeful gas pump, greeted you every fifty miles or so as you crossed the state. Between, the highway arced over pinyon-studded passes and raced through wide, gray valleys, moving in economically straight lines through a vast quiet. It was a road in a hurry to be someplace.

In the years before Gram died, we traveled Highway 50 once a summer with Aunt Anna. Aunt Anna would stuff us into the back seat of her Buick and head out at seventy mph, never speaking except to announce stops for gas, one eye on the road, one on the radio dial she twirled in an endless search through the static. We went east three times that I can remember, traveling to Salt Lake to see my aunts when they had babies. We traveled west more often. Some of my uncles lived in Reno. It was the more desirable destination. Gram loved to gamble in the big casinos, feeding silver dollars from her black purse into the slots with unflagging hopefulness. She was a cheerful loser, but a grim winner. She scooped her small jackpots into her purse and plowed towards the street.

I no dummy, mygolly. I quit when I head.

Leaving downtown Reno, she had Aunt Anna park on one of the bridges over the Truckee River. We'd stay for an hour or more while she sat in the middle of the back seat, arms crossed over her heavy purse, eyes darting to catch a glimpse of some movie star casting her wedding ring into the rushing water below.

You betcha my life, we see movie star today!

She was more successful as a gambler than as a sightseer.

Once at either of my uncles' houses, she established herself in the kitchen, taking over all the cooking while we were there. Between meals she poked through my uncles' vegetable gardens, shaking her head and muttering encouragement to the plants. On our long drive back to Taylor, she was antsy to be home again.

I never leave my little town again. I stay my little town. Everybody come me.

Traveling the desolate road home, I pointed out sights to distract her. There were four things to see along Highway 50 as it crossed the four hundred-mile width of Nevada. The first was her favorite, Sand Mountain. When it was miles behind us, she was still shaking with laughter and wiping tears from her cheeks. Sand Mountain was truly remarkable to see, but that wasn't why she loved it. She loved it because of the story, because it reminded her of my dad. She'd always look the other way, letting me be the first to point it out.

Look, Gram, I'd cue her. *Sand Mountain!*

Off to the left, a mountain of pure white sand reared into view, a mirage above the empty valley floor. A geological wonder, Sand Mountain rose nearly two thousand feet, every shimmering grain gathered by the wind from the beaches of a vanished sea. Travelers racing to and from California were drawn against their will to the side of the road, where they stood bare-headed and unbelieving in the midday sun.

My sonny boy, he say that mountain way over there in 1930.

Gram would point way off to the right of the road, beginning our beloved litany. It was a tall tale, full of reckless adventure and giant whoppers like a mountain of sand moving thirty miles. It was the closest we could get to my father. He had passed this way, in a Model A pickup, on his way to a Golden Gloves tournament in Reno. Eight teenagers filled the back of the truck. The coach drove. They ran up the passes and waited for the pickup to catch up, then barreled down the other side. My dad was the youngest, just thirteen. He had lied about Gram's permission and slipped away at night. He won his weight class, fighting against men twice his age. The coach gambled and lost every cent of his winner's purse. On the ride home, they stole green melons from a farmer's field to eat and were sicker than dogs. But Dad was flying. He was the undisputed king of clout. Right until the moment he stepped onto his own front porch. There was Gram with her old black frying pan and a clear suspicion of where he had been for the last three days. Dad grinned and shrugged. That wasn't why she hit him over the head. It was the nose. Along with the trophy and a set of tiny golden gloves to dangle from a key chain for a car that he never bought in his short life, Dad came home with a new nose, nearly flat and with a decided leftward leaning. For Gram, it was the last straw.

Jesus, Ma. Why ya hitting me? Ya coulda killed me. Aren't ya proud of your son? my dad asked as he picked himself off the front porch and rubbed his head. Gram shook the skillet in front of Dad's mangled face.

My son!? My son, he best nose whole family! Now look! You not so tough guy, buddy boy. You go shovel me coal.

Remembering Dad's short-lived title, Gram would shake her head and chuckle and wrap her arms around herself, holding the memory close to her heart, as if it were a young boy, battered, jubilant, and home at last.

Eventually, the open scenery would work on us. Gram would quiet as other memories collected her. Towards the middle of the state the ruins of a granite castle appeared to the right of the road, hunched on a high cliff overlooking the barren plain. Stokes Castle was angular and hollow, blue sky leaking through its bereaved windows. To Gram it was a giant grave marker, testament to the boom and bust of a long ago schemer, a miner and railroad man whose fortunes dried up when the gold played out. She would cross herself and then, nodding, make the motion of a small circle in the air in front of her.

Holy Wheel turn slowly, Mala. Better start at bottom, go just little bit up. Not so good have too much. Not so good be big shot at top.

Not far from the castle, too close if you wanted to savor your visual excitement, was a tiny, high valley, the third sight. Rich with hidden water, the little valley was a respite of green ringed with shivering aspens. Sometimes, waist-deep in waving reeds, deer or wild mustangs might raise their heads and acknowledge our passing.

Wish Taylor like this, Gram would murmur.

Long after the valley was lost behind us, we remembered the green. Then more sagebrush, more rocks, more dirt, another forlorn town or two, and, finally, on the loneliest part of the loneliest road in America, man-made piles of spent earth rose to block out the surrounding hills and told us we were nearly home. The huge tailings belonged to the Copper King open pit mine, one of the biggest in the world. This was the fourth sight along Highway 50, the reason for Parker's existence and our town's, too. The copper pit stood at the far edge of Parker. Highway 50 cut through the tailings piles on its way into town. Every day as the pit widened and deepened a little bit, the anemic tailings inched in on Parker a little more. We were vastly proud of the pit. Every old miner on every barstool in the county hooked a thumb in the direction of it and proclaimed, *I DUG THAT HOLE.* Standing on the edge of the enormous hole and looking down, it was hard to believe that anything human could have made it. But there they were, down in the bottom, men almost too small to see moving giant equipment too small for a child's hand. Ore cars circled slowly for more than an hour to reach the lip of the pit.

One day, break through, go down China, Gram would say.

I told her it was more likely the Indian Ocean.

Better! Then we have some pretty damn big lake. Then you see my garden!

She grinned at the thought. The highway followed the ore cars that left the pit and passed through Parker. Gram and I always checked the whorehouses at the end of town to see if we recognized any cars. Once past Parker, both the train tracks and the highway cut a straight line across the flat, dusty valley. Over the last thirty miles the limestone cliffs in front of us grew from bumps to mountains. These were my mother's cliffs, where she had tested the theory of flight. But that was a story that was never told, never whispered, ignored, a stranger's story. We moved on.

Where the cliff cast the longest shadow lay Taylor: a smokestack and a copper smelter, a ballpark, three churches, three shops, a garage, two bars, a barber shop, a bank, a post office, Mrs. Miniverri's In-home Diner, ten streets of picket fences, company houses, cottonwoods, and 1,822 people. Highway 50, *The loneliest road in America,* cut the town in half. Above Main lived the company managers, the businessmen and their wives, those Mormon mothers with their pale, blue-eyed children. Below Main were our people. We were home.

With its back against the cliffs, Taylor was hemmed in on the east by a cinder pile that threatened to engulf the Mormon Church. On the west a slag ditch rushed evil-looking, black muck down the tilting land from the smelter that crouched at the top of the town in the deep shadow of the cliffs. Below the town, the slag spread out and dried on a wide, acrid wasteland that we called The Sands. The name had an Arabian Nights air to it, romantic. We cherished little ironies. The Sands were home to tiny white scorpions and a particularly irritable species of rattler. Both were deadly. Taylor's sewer ran into the open slag ditch and out on to The Sands. Uncle Sam said Taylor was the only place in America where

14

you flushed it down your toilet in the morning and it blew back in your face in the afternoon. Sixth Street, where Gram and I lived (and Aunt Anna two doors down) was on the edge of The Sands. Most afternoons at about 2:00 the wind picked up in the northwest and a wall of dust swept across The Sands and moved in on the town. We watched it rolling toward our back fence. All over Taylor, laundry was snapped in. Children and pets scattered. Windows slammed shut. It was a good time to be at a friend's for a game of checkers, for a young wife to catch up on ironing, for old widows to share a cup of tea and a quiet gossip. It was a good time for a man to be at the Taylor Club with a foot on the rail and a whiskey in hand. It was a good time for stories. Each story shone. They massed into a mountain that shimmered, lighting our landscape.

In Taylor, days were the same, portioned by the smelter whistle at six, two, and ten, weighed in loaves of bread and glasses of whiskey, measured in deaths and stories. Time was unseen wind, rushing across plains, sharp and relentless, gathering debris and moving on.

By the summer that Gram died Taylor was drying up. Our last trips out of town to Salt Lake or Reno brought Gram, Aunt Anna, and me back to a town that was becoming the pallid leavings of what it had been. By 1950, most of the men and women who had been lucky enough to return from the war were moving away from Taylor. They had seen a world beyond the ten streets, the dust, the pit. The GI Bill opened a door they had never considered. The sons and daughters of immigrants were going to college. Added to this, another war had started. Taylor's mothers sent a second set of sons armed only with a confident swagger off to Korea. *Who would be left,* the circle of aging widow women wondered and watched with equal parts pride and sorrow as their sons and daughters left. My Aunt Anna knew. Bone stubborn, and insistent of one single truth, she knew Sixth Street, Taylor, Nevada, the street where she was born, where she bore her young, was the center of the universe. Roots and stories went as deep as the cottonwoods that shaded our sidewalks. It was meaning at the center of the mirage, a belonging passed down from Gram and the women of Taylor to everyone who once walked there.

Stay! Anna ordered.

It was hard not to listen to Anna. She was in charge. Only Gram could contradict her.

2

During the night that Gram died, all the cottonwoods in Taylor loosed their seed. In a mysterious collusion between Gram and nature, her old heart and the seedpods burst, releasing life at the same time. Like tiny, ghostly invaders, the cotton drifted along the moonlit streets of the town. Maybe it mingled there with Gram's newly freed spirit, and they settled down together to wait for the show to begin. It was a startling sendoff, beautiful, strange, funny. If Gram was indeed with us, in spirit, as well as deserted body, she enjoyed every minute of it. I know this. Even then, set adrift, tumbled with the pain and fear of being left behind, I could see it. It was one of the things she taught me.

It had been a winter of deep, wet snow. Early spring had brought historic rains that melted the snow pack and brought it rushing down the gullies. Parker, center of government, commerce, and sin for the county, had been two feet deep in brown water. Kids swept down Nevada Street wearing winter coats and riding inner tubes. Prostitutes on their own short street watched from balconies, cheering and offering cut-rate trade to volunteers from the copper smelter and the pit who were filling sandbags and trying to redirect the tide. So much water caused frantic activity and made instant heroes.

In our town, Taylor, the water rose around the roots of the cottonwoods. They were seldom swept away. Instead, the flood foretold a summer of plenty unheard of in that dry, dusty land. Heartwood pumped; sap ran thick. The trees set about the business of procreation. Three months later, in June, they set loose a monumental, record-breaking harvest of downy young.

That morning I woke to find my bedroom window screen transformed into a glowing, vibrating mat of white cotton. I called for Gram to come see, then jumped out of bed to look for her when she didn't answer. I thought she must be outside, uncovering her tender tomato plants. I didn't need to go that far to find her. She was slumped in the hall, four steps from my bedroom door, two steps from the bathroom, and six steps from the phone on the wall in the kitchen. I slid down the wall and sat next to her, drew her heavy, cold hand into my lap, wrapped my fingers around it. I worried about where she had wanted to go.

To me, I whispered and held on.

Last things hold importance to those left behind.

She was cool and firm under the thin material of her nightgown. Her flesh had already lost all memory of human response. Touching her, I knew everything that had been my grandmother had left. She had stepped out and away, leaving the heavy mantle of skin, the sturdy bones, the wrinkled, apple lady face with its crown of gray braids and all the old woman aches and pains that were part of the package. If Gram could have stood next to me looking down at that body, I know what she would have said, what she would have done. She would have shrugged her new, light shoulders and put an airy arm around me. *That okay maybe,* she would have said with her soft accent. *That lady, she pretty damn old.* She would have smiled at that, and added, *Time for her go, I guess.* She had always ended her most important pronouncements with *maybe* or *I guess*, then she'd shrug and smile and go on about her business. You had to wait patiently and listen closely to catch the few little truths she was willing to pass on. That was my job: to listen, to learn, to accept.

Not yet, I shook my head.

I traced the blunt fingers with my own, examined a nail chipped and tinged from gardening, a pinky finger more twisted and knobby than all the rest, a trace of flour still under its nail, on a palm a small nick, almost healed. I sat with her. I gathered to me all the previously unnoticed, and then put her hand in her lap, rose, and left her.

Running down Sixth Street for Aunt Anna, this new loss

18

filling me, I burst through warm, waist-high drifts of cotton dropped by the trees. It sifted from the clear sky, a mystical storm. The soft cotton caught the light breeze, flowed down the street, coating everything, clinging to the tops of my untied shoes, the front of my pajamas, my hair, and the salty wet of my cheeks. The world was awash in white. I couldn't tell whether the trees were weeping for my grandma's passing or dancing in joy for her release.

Gram would have loved her funeral. She was wearing a new pair of Uncle Milan's secret old lady shoes, which didn't happen often and always made her happy. It began as most funerals do with a gathering of family and friends, with sniffles, sobs, hugs, and fond memories. But, Gram's funeral, aided by her wild children and whipped up by an equally wild, strange, downy, summer blizzard, gained momentum and changed into something noisy, irreverent, and full of life. It ended in a grand, drunken celebration of Gram, of living in general, of anything else that could be safely toasted among the mixed populace of Serbs, Greeks, Italians, Basques, and the handful of real Americans privileged enough to be invited down to Sixth Street. There were spit-roasted pigs and lambs and enough alcohol to float the ark. The party lasted a day and a half, leaving the male residents of Sixth Street reeling and hiding from the sun for another week. It gave the widows and wives fuel for street-corner gossip for at least a month and enough ammunition against the male members of their extended families to ensure the completion of household projects for the next six. All in all, it was just what Gram would have wanted, what she deserved.

The funeral was held in the Church That Was Not Mormon and Was Not Catholic. It was an empty church on Main Street, once under the care of the Methodist Minister, but when his flock, a family of five, moved to Reno, it became known as the Church That Was Not Mormon and Was Not Catholic. In the same way the minister became know as the Methodist-

Minister-Without-A-Flock. Both were available for rental at a moment's notice. On this occasion, however, my Aunt Mary and Uncle Jo brought a borrowed Orthodox priest from some mountain monastery high above Salt Lake. He was Greek Orthodox and Gram was Serb, but she would not have minded, and neither did we. In his worn cassock and massive beard he looked authentically *Old Country*. His eyes streamed with real tears from the very beginning. Everyone was immediately impressed with his piety and wondered how much he had cost. He was allergic to the cottonwood seed. He wheezed and coughed through the long service, offering up in equal parts benedictions and sneezes. After some initial interest, his struggle went on almost unnoticed by his audience. I suspect the noise and inattention of the gathered mourners appalled him. In truth, we had drifted from the subject at hand, but Gram always hated being the center of attention. The old priest couldn't know we were paying tribute to Gram by being ourselves for her this one last time.

All of her scattered children and grandchildren were there. They bickered and teased one another. In the front pews, all my aunts by birth and marriage were arguing about whether it had been right to let Mr. Udiah Simple, the undertaker, apply makeup to Gram. There was no doubt, she now glowed in neon hues, a woman who had never worn anything on her face but a bit of olive oil to keep it soft and a generous coating of flour when she was baking. The debate flowed though the service; voices swirled and eddied through the stone halls. *Mama looks so nice! ...They shouldn't have put makeup on her. ...They do to make 'em look natural. ...Shhh! She never wore makeup a day in her life.... You can't look natural when you're dead. ...Shhh! ...They shouldn't have put that makeup on—she looks cheap! Shhh!! Do you think Mama cares right now whether she has makeup on or not?!? I say she looks cheap.... Say, Rosie, you should wear a little makeup—let your light shine.... Me? Go on!! ...Shh! She doesn't look cheap—you can't look cheap when you're lying in a coffin.... Kiki's right, Rosie, let your light shine! Shhh! C-H-E-E-P. Cheap! Yes, you could be very pretty with a little fixing up.... Shhh!! I don't think that's how you spell cheap.... Doesn't Mama look nice?....* My uncles dozed noncommittally or talked hunting and sports. A huge clot of grandchildren whispered, providing a palpable vibration that floated in the air above them as they squirmed in scratchy new dresses or clip-on ties.

There were friends and the children and grandchildren of friends who nodded and waved to each other, talking across the room in stage whispers. In the mid ground was a clutch of old women in their babushkas, sturdy shoes and perpetual black, the widows club, attending in strength, armed with clean hand-kerchiefs and damp eyes. Soon, tears gave way to gossip and arguments about past arguments. Babushkas nodded, eyes rolled. Scattered among the widows, under their wing, were the old miners and town oddballs, bachelors all. Like the rest of the sisterhood, Gram had fed them on homemade bread and soup. She had teased them until they smiled and sent them on their way. This was where Uncle Milan sat shyly watching the tips of Gram's new shoes, and where Peewee the Race Car Driver sat, whose strange injury from WWI made him seem always to be clutching a steering wheel and peering through the windshield of a speeding car. Here, too, was Gram's favorite, Naked Sal. Naked Sal had eluded his watchful, spin-ster sister. He arrived wailing with grief just after everyone had settled in. He wore only a thin coating of dust and a few sprigs of tumbleweed and cottonseed in his hair. His sister arrived shortly after, dressed him right there in the pew, boxed his ears and left, walking backwards and crossing herself repeatedly until she passed out the door of the church. The Methodist-Minister-Without-A-Flock sat next to Sal. He and Gram were gambling partners, pulling slot machine handles side by side every Saturday over in Parker after Gram's pension check came in. Sal gasped and blubbered, his tears leaving shiny,

21

pink stripes on his dirty face. The Methodist-Minister-Without-A-Flock patted Sal's back and took the opportunity to practice a bit with an impromptu sermon for the distraught old man. The sound level rose and fell, then built new strength, and each time the priest sneezed a ripple ran through the gathered multitude as we all crossed ourselves in unison. Perhaps we were listening a bit after all.

In front of us, no doubt quietly enjoying the show, Gram reigned serenely, the tip of her nose glowing with Mr. Simple's No. 3 Pink and the tips of her new shoes winking in the candle light from the altar.

On the shoulders of my uncles, Gram's casket passed down the aisle, out the door, and down the steps to the hearse waiting in a street liquid with shifting drifts of cottonseed. Behind the wheel, Mr. Simple turned the key and pressed on the gas pedal. But the hearse responded with a gasp and wheeze reminiscent of our rented priest. Its air intake was clogged. So uncles and cousins, friends and neighbors gathered around the stricken hearse and began to push. In dark suits and dresses and our best shoes we pushed Gram down Main Street. Gaining speed as we passed the diner, the shops, the theater, the barber shop, the Taylor Club, and the post office, we sailed out of town, down the quarter mile of Highway 50, through the gates of Taylor Cemetery and up the dusty, rutted track to the grave site. Those who couldn't find a spot to push trotted behind. Gram rode in style.

In the cemetery, the cotton leaped and spun in the wind, gathered in clumps, tumbled haltingly through the sparse grass to congregate against the tombstones. Gram's grave had completely filled with it. The priest was so overcome with sneezing that his benediction was a series of frantic arm-waving and heroically suppressed eruptions. His beard was woven with cottonseed. My Aunts Mimi and Kiki kept reaching over to brush it off in hopes of helping him. They succeeded in sending more of it up his nose. Silently, we all wagered whether he would make it through to the end. With a great deal of eye rolling and winking, Uncle Mike and Uncle Sam stationed themselves at the near corners of the grave, prepared to catch the priest if a sudden fit should send him face-first into the soft, white bed at his feet. A final enormous sneeze sent him not forwards as predicted, but backwards where no one waited to catch him. It was the right moment to call it quits. We all hollered together, *Amen!* The coffin was lowered into the grave.

The coffin's bulk displaced the trapped cotton, which reared up in a wide, white column. It caught the wind, pushed through the gathered crowd, and rushed to join a dust devil forming in the ruts of the cemetery road. My aunts gathered around the fallen priest. My uncles shoveled dirt into the grave. The dirt clods made a hollow, empty sound as they landed on the pale oak of the coffin. I turned to watch the tight, new-formed whirlwind. Tiny filaments caught the sun, shooting out sparks of light. The cotton joyously twisted and weaved and rose. A white, living thing. It danced mid-air with rapturous freedom. A careless scattering of twigs and last year's leaves marked its dusty, arcing passage. Pausing in a wide, flat, sun-lit space, its shimmering sides expanded as if taking a deep breath. Gaining height and strength and resolve, it swept down the cemetery road and out onto the highway.

I said good-bye. Bon voyage.

3

Poker. While we played it out in Aunt Anna's garage, in the house the adults drank, bargained over who would keep me, and listened to my cousin Josie. Called from our game, she played to requests on her accordion, sad Serb songs and lively polkas. It was the second night of Gram's wake. About twenty cousins and assorted neighborhood friends between six and eighteen years of age stuffed the corrugated iron garage on the edge of The Sands. The back end was buried in sand and dirt and tumbleweeds, giving it the damp, secret quality of a cave. Tiny cones of dust scattered around the dirt floor testified to every slight chink in the garage's armor. A pinball machine, an ancient, dusty couch and a pool table balanced on thin slats of wood made it the favored hideout of the Sixth Street kids. We had been sitting or standing around the pool table for three hours, playing seven-card draw with three decks shuffled together, jokers, one-eyed jacks, suicide kings, and twos all wild. It was an exciting game, possible to have a hand of seven aces. Twelve of us were playing, the rest providing an expert, running commentary. We were all penniless, so my cousin Steve had brought an old atlas down from the house. Each of us had part of a continent. We bet mountain ranges and cities, natural resources, whole countries. No one kept track of winnings, but all knew when someone tried to bet something already lost. It was a loud game, helped along by cokes, chocolate cake and a smuggled Ball jar of Eli's wine. We were gambling with the world. My world.

Josie came through the door of the garage with her accordion draped over her shoulder.

Well, she announced to the crowd, *she's staying with us.* Josie heaved the accordion into the air. It sailed, sighing, over our heads and landed on the couch with a human complaint.

Not in our room, retorted Paul. He already shared the back bedroom with his two brothers and Sofie, his sister.

Well, not mine either, kids, stated Josie flatly. As the oldest, she had a room to herself, the back porch. Cool and breezy in the summer, thick ice formed on the inside of its windows in October and finally melted in late May. The winter wind rattled the windows, creating spider webs in the ice. To reach the back steps and the yard below, everyone in the house squeezed past the end of her bed and opened the door with a loud crack against her chest of drawers. Even so, it was heaven to Josie. She would only be in the room another few months before she went East to college, but the room was hers. Alone. Sofie counted the days until it passed down to her.

Guess it's the front room couch for you, Mala, said Sofie, as she deftly dealt another hand of stud.

She could stay out here, someone suggested. To everyone present, sleeping on a sloping couch in the constant presence of a pool table and pinball machine seemed preferable to being under the baleful eye of Aunt Anna.

No such luck. Ole Nick sleeps it off here when Mom won't let him in, said Paul of his father, then added, *Three*, and slapped some cards down on the felt.

She'll make you learn an instrument, my friend Carrie warned. Everyone in the room shuddered. Aunt Anna made sure her children were musical. She pulled them out and displayed them at every family gathering, much to the adults' enjoyment, the cousins' amusement, and the performers' humiliation. Josie played the accordion, Paul the trumpet and trombone, Luke and Eddy the guitar and mandolin. Every morning, they practiced in the kitchen while Aunt Anna stirred eggs or oatmeal in time.

My cousin Sofie had managed to out-fox her mom. She played the piano. There wasn't room for one in the house, so each afternoon Aunt Anna escorted her to Kiki and Mimi's house to practice. Anna couldn't stand her sisters, Kiki and

Mimi. She loved them. She would defend them against hoards of Turks without being asked. She just couldn't be near them. They talked too much. She called them Heckle and Jeckle after the crows in the cartoon. She wouldn't step foot in their house. Sofie's aunts ushered her in from the front porch. She sat on the couch and was fed Greek cookies and milk for fifty-five minutes, Kiki and Mimi talking, talking, talking. Five minutes before the hour was up, Sofie moved from the couch to the piano stool, played "Beautiful Dreamer" twice, and then waited for her mom to bang on the front door. When Aunt Anna showed up, Kiki and Mimi were non-stop, stereo praise.

So talented. Yes, talented. She gets better every day. Don't you think so? Oh, I do, I do! She plays like an angel. Yes, and so pretty! Oh, very pretty. "Beautiful Dreamer" is our favorite, you know. Yes, our absolute favorite. Isn't it, Mimi? Oh, yes Kiki! It is! She'll be on the stage, don't you think, Mimi? Oh, I do, Kiki! I do! We'll be so proud. We'll tell everyone we know her! Yes, we'll tell everyone! Won't that be fun? Oh yes, Kiki. Such fun! She's talented. Yes very talented!

Kiki and Mimi rarely required a response, so Aunt Anna simply dragged Sofie down the street in wrathful silence, while Kiki and Mimi sent a shock wave of admiration and loving farewells rolling after them. Whenever there was a piano present at a family function, Sofie regaled the crowd with "Beautiful Dreamer" to the great appreciation of everyone. Aunt Anna's smile was a bit tight at the corners. She harbored suspicions.

There aren't many instruments left, one of my younger cousins pointed out, worried it might be a condition of living here.

Mala can learn the violin, another suggested. *One card.*

No! The tuba! Everyone laughed.

There hadn't really been any question where I would end up living. Aunt Anna was the undisputed monarch of the family. She wasn't the oldest. She was the toughest. Years before,

Gram had gathered her boys around her and told them, *When I gone, you listen Anna. She know best. You be sure listen Anna.* Gram recognized in Anna a will smelted to metal, knew her daughter's determination to hold everything together with her own hands. The family did what Gram told them. Now they did what Anna told them. On the second night of the wake, Anna told them I was staying with her, on Sixth Street, in Taylor. Of course they all offered anyway. It had been nice to hear the words over the past few days. *Why don't you come home with us? ...Come stay. ... California's nice. ...Come to Salt Lake with us. ...You like Reno. ...We have plenty of room! ...Just come home with us. ...We'd love to have you.* Even Kiki and Mimi pulled me aside, whispering, *Mimi and me want you to stay with us...yes, Mala, stay with Kiki and me...if Anna says so...she might say yes...she might....* They threw glances toward the kitchen where Aunt Anna was banging pots.

Now, every eye in the dusty garage was on me, waiting for some response.

I'd like to play the flute, I murmured, looking down at my hand. Not a single wild card. I set my cards down on the table. *I fold.*

The couch in Aunt Anna's front room wasn't bad. My suitcase fit underneath, so no one tripped. The problem was, I couldn't seem to stay put. I always started out on the couch, the quilt clutched around me, my head angled up against the arm rest, but somehow I woke up in my own bed in Gram's house without any memory of having traveled the short strip of street to get there. There I'd be, my own patch of early sun warming my face and waking me to air rich with the scent of baking bread.

Gram? I'd call and trail into the kitchen.

The kitchen was empty, cold and clean. It held the smell of baking bread, but not in the same way as my dream. The odor was faint, as if this was a place where bread had once been made often and lovingly, but now only the walls and the table

27

were left to hold the slight scent of memory. I could have made the bread myself, pulled out the flour, salt and sugar, set milk on the stove to warm and dissolve the yeast. I knew it all by heart, but bread was made to share. So, I'd just boil water for tea, waiting at the table for Aunt Anna's arrival. Soon she'd be standing in the doorway, hands on her hips, head shaking. *Come on,* she'd say. As I passed her, she'd grab me and hug me, kiss my head, then pull me down the street by my pajama collar. She didn't ask me why I did it, or how long I was planning on continuing. Aunt Anna never asked a question if she couldn't argue with the answer and win.

I had been staying at Aunt Anna's twelve days when Uncle Nick came back. Gram's wake had inspired him. He had decided to go on one of his periodic jaunts and do some serious drinking. No one knew where he went, but it was farther than the Taylor Club or even Parker. Aunt Anna didn't look in the bars there anymore. She didn't look at all. Maybe he went to Elko, maybe Battle Mountain, maybe as far as Chicago for all anyone knew. He'd be gone anywhere from a few days to a week or more. No one ever worried. He always came home: empty-handed, stinking, and sorry. Gram had never been very impressed with Nick. She called him *That Nogood SonnaMaBitch.* I was nine before I realize it wasn't his name. She'd always add after some thought, *At least That Nogood SonnaMaBitch no beat my Anna.* Considering Aunt Anna, it wasn't a likely worry.

Everyone else was in bed. I was listening to the wind in the cottonwoods and waiting to fall asleep when I heard the front door knob rattle. We didn't lock our doors in Taylor. Anna only did to keep Uncle Nick out. I could hear him shuffle around the side of the house and clump up the back stairs. He tried Josie's door. He was loud enough to wake her, but Josie wasn't budging.

The next I heard from Uncle Nick, he was at Aunt Anna's bedroom window, scratching at the screen. *Hooonnneeeey,* he crooned in the low, plaintive wail of a coyote. Far off down the street a dog whined. Aunt Anna was silent. *Hooonnneeeey, please. Nick loves you! Let me in. I show you.*

I could hear the bedsprings complain on the other side of the wall from my couch. Aunt Anna was sitting up in bed. I couldn't see it, but I knew she was crossing steel arms against her chest. *Nick loves you!* she mimicked. *You shit!*

Honey. Anna. I do love you. I do! Let me in. I show you. Uncle Nick's voice was tinged with a panicked bravado now. He didn't like the garage on the cusp of The Sands, its cold couch and the company of the pool table. *Anna, please. I so sorry!*

The bed springs complained again, and Aunt Anna's feet slapped the floor and stomped to the window. The window scraped, and the screen hit the floor. *Get in here you damn fool. You'll wake the whole street*, she hissed. *Jesus H. Christ!* she muttered, stomping back to bed.

Anna honey, Uncle Nick puffed as he forced himself through the window. He must have landed on the floor with his face. There was a muffled *Oof*, and then groans and scrabbling as limbs untangled and hoisted themselves upward to stand. Hopping and grunting suggested his clothes gave him a good struggle, but finally they hit the floor clump by clump. Aunt Anna heaped grumbled curses on him while he worked. The bed groaned one last time. I turned over and closed my eyes.

The headboard gave a soft, insistent knock against the wall.

Anna, you so beautiful, Uncle Nick mumbled. *You sweet. I swear you, I never go again.*

Oh, you damn fool, Aunt Anna murmured again, her voice low. The wall began to shiver from a slow, rhythmic thumping. I pulled the quilt over my head.

Thump...Thump...

I sat up on the couch.

Thump...

Something lightly hit the top of my head and dropped into

29

my lap. I picked it up and looked at it closely in the gloom, a puzzle piece. Above me the framed, 1,000-piece puzzle of Niagara Falls that hung over the couch trembled, stilled, trembled, stilled...

Standing on the couch I examined the puzzle in the dark. Fifteen pieces were missing.

Thump...thump...

I tried to remember how long the puzzle had been hanging. Five years, fifteen pieces...

Thump...

Oh, for Christ's sakes! growled a voice behind me, interrupting my calculations. Josie was standing in her babydolls in the doorway between the kitchen and the front room.

We stared at each other, listening.

Another puzzle piece popped off the wall and hit me in the back of the head, tangled itself in my hair. I pulled it out, looking at it with confusion. Sixteen pieces?

Thump...thump...

That's it, Josie grimly dragged me from my balance on the couch. She propelled me through the front door, leaving it wide open, and marched me determinedly down the street. The wind pushed at our backs. Gram's front gate banged behind us, smacking us into the front yard. Inside, Josie hurried me into bed. Tall and spare, bending to me, she pressed the cover down around, securing me there in my bed. Her long, dark hair brushed my face, the touch of a ghost.

Go to sleep now, Mala. I'll be right in the back bedroom.

I heard her stop in the bathroom opposite Gram's room, then move into the kitchen and the room in back where one or another aunt or uncle would crowd with their family when they came to visit.

Away from Anna's...home...not alone. I slept.

Next morning, I put on Gram's apron and made bread, pogacha, squat and heavy and gold. Perfect, like Gram's. In the big bowl, I sifted flour, salt, and sugar with my fingers. Shaping a cone, I dented the top and poured the warmed milk and yeast into the crater. Using my hands and shoulders I worked the dough, then smoothed the ball and rolled it in olive oil. I set it on the kitchen table in the sun to rise just once and a little more. Josie woke to the smell of bread baking.

Jesus, Mala, I didn't know you could do this. I didn't think I'd ever taste pogacha like this again, she said after her first chewy mouthful. Butter melted over the thick slice and pooled in her cupped hand. We sipped tea and smiled silently at each other over chipped china.

Aunt Anna was an hour and ten minutes late. The front gate banged, the doorknob jiggled, then a fist pounded. *Josie! Mala! The door's locked!*

Josie lifted her head and raised her eyebrows. *Who's there?* she called pleasantly from the kitchen table.

The silence on the other side of the front door was so long, the weight of it pulled my throat tight. I couldn't swallow the tea cooling in my mouth. Josie blew gently on her tea, watching the vapor billow lazily away from her. The front gate banged. I jumped, gulping tepid saliva and tea. Josie dipped her head, slowly drawing in the fragrant breath of her slice of bread, quietly contemplating the unexpected perfection of it.

We were staying.

4

I spent my days with ghosts. The minute Josie left for work they glided from closets and slipped from underneath beds to keep me company. Gram's house, Gram's ghosts. They whispered the story of her life. She lived a long time and buried a lot of people she had loved. I was her last unlooked-for child, brought to her by the death of her son, kept near her till her own death. With food and love and a home she had also offered the distilled liquid of her life. I knew the taste of her gains and losses, and had seen in her the reflection of faces left behind. I was the keeper of Gram's house and of her memory.

When she had left the village outside Zagreb to follow her young husband to America, she had left two small children behind. The plan had always been to gather enough money to bring them over, but it had never happened. In this new country there were new babies, babies that came almost every year for more than twenty years. The struggle to feed and clothe the ones around her widened the world between her and those first two. There was no word of them. No one she knew from the Old Country could read or write. She was hardly better off. Time conspired with circumstance and the chorus of upturned mouths. She mourned those first two in quiet moments, kneading bread in a pre-dawn kitchen, pulling in lines of clothes, folding sun-warm trousers, small undershirts, knotting worn socks, placing them carefully into her basket. But she remembered them at all times, the two small faces, pale under shocks of black hair, framed by a receding window. The image fixed forever onto her vision the moment she turned and walked down the hill from her brother's house a world away and a lifetime ago. She remembered the weight of the bundle in her arms and what it carried—spare clothes, two cooking pots, candles, a small bag of coins.

There were other children, too, an infant boy and a five-year-old girl lost in the flu epidemic of 1918. They were buried in Pennsylvania. Then, in Colorado, Gram buried her first husband, the father of her first ten children. He died from silicosis, "miner's consumption."

In 1944, Gram learned that another child, my father, had died on the beaches at Normandy. I was seven. He had been away two and a half years. My memories were more of movement and sound, a presence quick and sure, than of an actual man. I gauged my loss by Gram's reaction of quiet tears and acceptance, and by the reaction of the rest of the family and the town: utter disbelief. Even though his body lay under a neat white cross on a quiet seaside hill in France, he was still everywhere in our town. His boxing gloves hung in the Pool Hall alongside the Golden Gloves trophy. You could feel the weight of them if you liked, slip your hands into the cool interior and feel the padding mould your fingers into fists. In the halls of Parker High School his trophies filled cabinets: track, basketball, baseball, and football. Down at the Taylor Club there were trophies too, town league baseball mostly. There was a picture of him recovering a grounder, a picture of him beginning his swing at a fast ball that streaks across the picture in a smear of white, and about half a dozen shots of him with his grinning teammates, state champions. Kitty corner to this shrine there was a war wall. He was there, too, his familiar squashed nose and jutting chin among faces of others either dead or heroes or both. The old miners who line the benches outside the club would stop me and tell me stories about my dad, his pranks, his triumphs, the way he and his pals crowded into a box car and fought bare knuckled in the pitch black. *Just for hell of it*, they'd say and laugh their hoarse, coughing laugh and shake their heads. Only my dad walked out unscathed, chin up and grinning into the bright sunlight. Indomitable. How could someone like that step onto a beach in a far country and simply drop dead from one well-placed bullet? It couldn't be! Gram knew better.

33

At home a picture of him hung directly above the dip in the couch that Gram and I had formed by years of close sitting. We listened to the radio, I read to her, and she talked, recounting her life. Above us, the portrait of Uncle Sam, Dad, and Uncle Mike leaned forward from its nail. They smiled eagerly from sharp-angled, Slavic faces. Their tinted eyes looked beyond our perch on the couch. Their hats were set at rakish angle. They were ready for a fight.

When my dad died, I read the telegram. Gram took it from me and collapsed into the dip in the couch gazing up at the picture, silent tears running down her face and drowning the thin slip of paper in her hands. Eli, Gram's second husband and father to her last six children, struggled out of his armchair and clumped over to her, thumping her rhythmically on her back until she became sensible of the pain. She patted his knee once, wiped her eyes, and went into the kitchen to make his lunch. It was the first bit of affection I had ever seen Eli show towards Gram. Stunned, I scuttled after Gram, afraid I might have a share of his sympathy. They were fighting again by sundown.

Eli died three years later. It took us half the day to notice he was dead, sitting in his chair with his stiff leg positioned just where it would cause the most trouble. We had only thought him unusually quiet, a little less cantankerous than normal. When Gram called him to dinner at five, he didn't respond. She came in from the stove and smacked him across the head, calling irritably, *Get up, Old Man!* She stepped back, grinning, to wait for his growled curse and the swing of his cane. At the blow, his head flopped forward, and his glasses dropped from his nose. For the space of two minutes Gram stood staring down on Eli's slumped body. She let out a deep, angry wail and smacked his unresisting head, one last time, getting in the last word. Then she stepped over his leg, pushed through the front door, sat down with a thump on the front step, threw her apron over her head and began to keen. I went into the kitchen to take the pork chops off the stove, then came to join her on the step.

34

I never marry no more, she wailed, shaking her head violently. *Men just plain no good!*

Even if you wanted to, Gram, I said, trying to cheer her up, *The pickings are getting kinda slim...*

From underneath her apron, Gram wailed again. I put my arms around her and rocked with her, caught in the rhythm of her grief and disappointment. In my mind a meandering line grew, men, gray, stooped, tottering like an ancient picket fence. They shuffled forward in time to our rocking. In front, Gram stood, feet planted, arms crossed over her best church dress. She examined them as if they were used plates at a fire sale, squinting, checking for flaws. *Nosireebob,* she'd say, shaking her head grimly, *I never marry no more!* In turn, each old man shrugged stiff hunched shoulders and wandered off, seamlessly replaced by the next hopeful suitor. As it turned out, Gram didn't need a new man. It was hard to kick a habit of twenty-five years. Gram continued to argue with Eli, to make his favorite meals, and to cuss his empty chair until the day she died.

Keep a-goin, that's what Gram said if anyone asked how she was doing. That's how she moved through the deep waters of her life. She never asked it of others, never expected it, but it is what she always hoped for.

It was Gram's absence that haunted the house. Her slippers still waited by her bed, her apron still hung on the doorknob of the back door, her bottles and lotions still made a short, neat line along the bathroom cabinet. Alone, I could curl up on her bed and press my face into her pillow and almost catch the powdery nearness of her. I could open her drawers and trace the patterns of her winter stockings, alive with bold color. I could count her hundred white handkerchiefs, each embroidered with a long-remembered woodland flower, each hemmed, ironed, folded, and stored, neat piles of delicate prayers. I could pull her apron off the doorknob and put it on, stand at the counter and gather the ingredients for dinner

35

around me. As I chopped or stirred or kneaded dough, I almost felt her knowing hands with their crooked, roughened fingers melt into mine and we were one…almost. Her absence was huge in the tiny house; there was hardly room for the rest of us, the ghosts and me. Transparent, we crowded in the corners and skirted the edges of rooms, looking for a comfortable spot to land.

Only Josie could cut through the thick air of the house like a new, sharp knife. She didn't recognize ghosts, didn't follow rules. When she left for work, rushing because she was late, she'd brush by Eli's armchair and step right on the spot where his stiff leg used to thrust out and down from his throne, blocking the path to the front door. She did it every morning. In the evenings, relaxed and a day richer, she'd open wide the front door and sweep in, drawing with her the evening air and the grape pop smell of blooming Russian olives.

Mala, I'm here, she'd call.

Coming from the kitchen, I'd find her flopped down in Eli's chair, a high-heeled shoe in each hand. Behind her I could almost see Eli, stiff with shock and affront, adjusting his tiny spectacles with jerking fingers, unsure what to do about this teenage granddaughter sprawled barefoot in his lap. No one sat in Eli's chair. Gram or I had spent the three years since his death perched gingerly on its wide arm when guests came and inhabited our couch. There was a wide worn spot just the size of her ample rump. Sometimes we pulled chairs in from the kitchen, and Eli's armchair remained majestically empty. In and out of the door a hundred times a day, we always sidestepped where Eli's leg had been, remembering the *Watch leg!* he used to bark from the recesses of his throne and the threatening swipe of his cane. Without even realizing they did it, all of our visitors sidestepped Eli's leg, too. They had been visiting long before the leg and its man vacated. They did it out of habit, out of respect. Habit and respect, these were what Sixth Street ran on. Josie had neither.

My dad's shortstop mitt had always inhabited the house. It showed up in the crook of the couch, on the kitchen table, or on the edge of the bathroom sink, as if it still traveled every day to the ballpark then back home where it rested in spots easily to hand. Gram and I had negotiated around the rhythm of its comings and goings. Josie was forever sweeping it aside to make room for her morning newspaper and cup of tea, pulling the battered old glove from the corner of the couch, carelessly tossing it off into some less traveled spot, only to find it beneath her as she sat down later. The mitt was persistent, like Eli's leg, like each unused item that whispered of absence: the slippers, the pillow, the hundred neatly folded handkerchiefs. Each laid its claim, calling for the habit of use, the respect of notice. I could be persistent, too. We needed a home, a family, Josie...

Keep a-goin, I could almost hear Gram urge. *Keep a-goin.*

5

At first Aunt Anna just called, offering weather predictions as if two doors down was a world away, announcing the menu for the day and ending the largely one-sided conversation with an oblique, *I make enough food to feed anyone in this town. I never turn a hungry mouth away from the table. That's all I'll say.* Click.

Then one night, Uncle Nick showed up at the door on his way home from the barbershop. He still wore his white barber's shirt with its dusting of hair: gray, black, brown, a few blond highlights. Aunt Anna had probably said, *You bring those girls home tonight for dinner, or don't come home yourself!* So there he stood on the front porch, head down, shifting from foot to foot. Milan stood beside him, silent support.

Nick and Milan were a package deal; that's what Aunt Anna called them. They had been born in Taylor, but sent back to the Old Country with their mother when they were still little. Their dad loved the ladies. He wanted room to work. Not too long after, he was shot dead halfway out someone else's bedroom window, but Nick and Milan didn't come back until they were adults, no longer American, never quite Serb. Nick gained enough English to propose to Anna. Milan never did master English. Anna took over talking for both of them. They had little to say for themselves after that. Nick and Milan were famous. Nick for the precision of his haircuts and for wandering off to drink for days and sometimes weeks, leaving the town's hair to grow unchecked. Milan was known as the man whose shoes Patton died in. He had remade his army boots in basic training. They were quickly confiscated and then slowly made their way up the military hierarchy as they chased Hitler's troops across Europe. Someone said they saw the boots on Patton's feet in Berlin. History. After the war, back in Taylor, Milan mended soles and worn-down heels, and in the quiet, dim space of his shop he crafted secret widow's shoes for every old woman on Sixth Street. Shoes, black and sturdy, with prim leather laces, which were perfect replicas of the ones these women had left their homelands in. He kept charts of the old ladies' feet, maps of every tender defect. He stole into bedrooms heavy with drifting memories and sleep and slipped the shoes beneath soft dust ruffles. The toes, still damp with polish, peeked out to greet the widows with the morning light. We all knew he did it. We didn't let on. He didn't need the thanks, wouldn't want the notice. Milan lived for the shoes. With Nick, his brother, fellow refugee and quiet companion, and the shoes to feed his soul, Milan was complete. Anna took care of the rest.

Standing now, shoulder to shoulder, without Anna to push them from behind, they couldn't quite bring themselves to their task.

Well? Josie prompted.

Are you hungry? Uncle Nick asked hopefully by way of an opening. His eyes never left the welcome mat.

No, Josie said through the screen door. Uncle Nick's shoulders rose and dropped. Hair sprinkled down around him. Milan shook his head sadly.

He tried again. *See... Well, your mom... Anna thought... she said... dinner... I bet it's gonna be good...* he trailed off in wistful incoherence and sighed again.

Josie stared at him hard-eyed for a moment. *Are _you_ hungry?* she asked at last.

Well... I... yes...

Come on in you two, Josie said. *We were just about to sit down. You might as well have something to eat before you're denied your own dinner. Mala's made lamb chops and potatoes. There's plenty.* She opened the screen door wide and pulled them through, brushing the hair from Uncle Nick's shoulders as he stepped over the threshold.

I love lamb, he said shyly. *Maybe just a little bite for the walk home,* he added sheepishly. Milan nodded.

Sure, Josie laughed. *You could use some fortifying! Mala, go down to the cellar and get one of Eli's jars of wine. We'll fix you right up.*

The next morning a new pair of sandals lay on the welcome mat, hand-sewn and still smelling of leather oil. Josie examined them.

Nice. Not my size, she grinned. *They must be for the cook.*

Aunt Anna sent Mimi and Kiki next. They came while Josie was at work. Josie frightened them almost as much as Aunt Anna. They sat on the couch, their thighs touching, sipping coffee in unison. Their heads bobbed. Their eyes blinked.

This is such a nice house. Don't you think so, Kiki?

Oh yes! So nice! Quiet, too. A nice quiet house, Mimi. I love this house.

Do you love this house, Mala?

Yes, Aunt Kiki. I love this house.

I bet Josie loves this house, too. Does she, Mala?

Yes, Aunt Mimi, she does.

Yes, we were sure she did, weren't we, Kiki?

We were, Mimi. Pause. The quiet house was quieter for a moment.

Everybody loves this house. All of Mama's children love this house.

We do, Kiki! All of us. Anna loves this house. Doesn't she Kiki?

She does, Mimi... Aunt Kiki's voice trailed off. The nice, quiet house was silent for fully three minutes.

Well, we should be going, Mimi. Don't you think?

Oh yes, Kiki. We should go. We have so much to do, don't we?

Oh, so much! Their heads bobbed in unison as they hustled out of their seats and handed me cups of half-finished coffee.

We could come back, though, couldn't we, Kiki?

What a nice idea, Mimi! Could we do that, Mala?

Yes, Aunt Kiki. You can always come back.

Oh good! Isn't that good, Mimi?

Oh yes! We just love this house. Don't we Kiki?

We do. It's such a nice quiet house. We love you, too, Mala. Don't we, Mimi?

We do! They kissed me, hugged me, kissed me again and then bobbing, they backed out the screen door. Outside on the porch, they stopped and checked the street. In a stage whisper:

Maybe it's best not to tell Anna.

No, no, Kiki. You're right. We don't want to bother Anna.

No, let's not bother Anna. She's so...busy. It can be our little secret.

Mimi! A wonderful idea! Our little secret! Anna is...busy.

Okay, I smiled. *Our little secret.*

Mimi and Kiki crept out the front gate and scurried the wrong way down the street. They didn't want to cross by Aunt Anna's house. Their backs bent, their heads and shoulders pressed together, like two small creatures rushing home with a shared burden, the heavy weight of deception and relief.

Mimi and Kiki were my favorite aunts. I loved their twin, lacquered hairdos and their bright black eyes. They had always been Gram's favorite, I suspect, though she would have never said so. She took great pleasure in simply watching them as they sat and chirped at her from the couch. They had no father. They arrived mysteriously in the time between when Gram had lost her first husband and hadn't met her second. Their tiny faces were long and dark, distinctly Greek-looking, which could have pointed to half the men in town, but Gram wasn't telling. When one or two of the wives demanded whose husband it had been, Gram had shrugged and said *Maybe no husband...maybe miracle. Children always miracle.* She jabbed a finger at heaven and grinned. For most of the women on Sixth Street it wasn't much more than a point of curiosity. As the years went by it mattered less and less. The circle they formed was more important than the inexplicable rhythms their men danced to around its edges.

There were other emissaries who visited. Naked Sal came to the front gate. Next to him stood the Methodist-Minister-Without-a-Flock, looking anxious. I invited them in. Sal, used to the hospitality of Gram's kitchen and the feel of the smooth, cool wood of her kitchen chair under his dusty rump, would have obliged, but the Minister held him back. He cleared his throat and said in his best pulpit voice:

We are on an errand of mercy, Miss Mala. Your Aunt has sent us. She thinks you and your cousin Josie should go home.

Thank you, Minister, Mr. Sal, but I am home. You sure you won't come in and have something to eat?

They wouldn't stay. Having said what they were sent to say, they left, walking down the street side by side, the minister looking overdressed next to Sal, who wore nothing more than a tan, a modest covering of grime, and a vacant grin. They walked in the direction of Mrs. Miniverri's, who was just then serving lunch in her In-home Diner. For the Methodist-Minister-Without-a-Flock and Naked Sal meals were always free.

As Aunt Anna spread word of our defection, along Main Street knots of old women clutching bags of groceries gathered like crows to corn to discuss the matter. When they showed up at our door, they came out of curiosity, wondering how we'd do, Josie and I, two girls 18 and 13, without the sheltering wing of Anna. Could we keep the house clean? Who would do the laundry? What would we eat? They hadn't reckoned on Josie's determination or my hard work. They hadn't reckoned with themselves, either. Each time they came, they brought something. *Just a little soup, chicken, just right for you...You maybe want some beans, just little beans...You take this pork with sauerkraut, so nice for you...I bring you some ravioli, not too much, just a little, I make too much, I give you some...I bring nice roast for you, potatoes too....* When they stood to leave that first time, slowly, gingerly, they shook arthritic fingers at me in cursory disapproval, *Mala, you take Josie go home Anna now. You starve here all alone!* They were not worried. Behind each of them stretched a history of leaving home, learning, making do, standing alone.

Soon, the hunched, carefully stepping figures came every day. They held warm treasure protectively to their chests and watched the deceptive pavement for wayward stones and errant cracks. Curiosity brought them to me; habit made them stay. They had been making this short trek for over forty years. The fact of Gram's death could have little effect on the simple, daily movements of a lifetime. Sometimes there were only one or two of them. Sometime the front room bristled with scratchy black wool and nodding gray heads. I took to making sheet cakes and big pots of tea. *Have a little cake...*Gram's voice woven through my own. They sat with their pale plates in the wide, flat expanse of their black laps. They teased one another until the room filled with the sound of their chortling, cackling laughter. Tears ran down the seams of their faces, and as one they pulled daintily worked handkerchiefs from between heavy bosoms and mopped their faces, then shook their fists at one another and started off again.

They exchanged symptoms like recipes and examined each other's illnesses with equanimity, offering home cures they all knew anyway. It wasn't long before I knew all their bowel habits, their aches and pains, the dreams that woke them in the night, holding them wide-eyed in their beds until dawn, remembering. I learned that warmed olive oil with a hint of cayenne eased stiff joints, a shot of whiskey after dinner kept you regular, and that tears were the best cure for cloudy vision. I learned there was no cure for dreams or memories.

This medical discussion was their opening affirmation, a litany repeated for decades, comforting in its sameness. Then, done with diseases for the day, they gossiped, sometimes giggling like children, sometimes sadly crossing themselves, kissing their fingers and making the sign of the Holy Wheel in the charged air they shared. Here was their religion, shaped in the shared space on this short street of this small town. A religion they had pulled together from scraps of what each had brought from diverse foreign lands, what they learned along the way, what they saw around them every day and, above all, what they hoped: that the mighty fall, the lowly rise, rise, rise. The trick was to watch quietly and pray openly and hope you were on the side of the Wheel that was headed up in its certain, slow roll of fate and justice and God. Before me every house in town opened, revealing its fragile seed and the tendrils of hidden roots that marked its tenuous spot on the Wheel. I heard about the grocer's secret heart condition and the banker's wife who let the older Vaccari brother in through the bedroom window for the short half hour that lay between the end of the three o'clock shift and the bang of the kitchen door announcing that her two children were home from school. I now knew that Mrs. Whitacker, the smelter manager's wife, had the biggest feet in town and drank gin like a fish every afternoon when the dust kicked up. I learned that Mary Ualdivich, from the switch- board, had a lump the size of an old lady's fist right here between her breast and armpit. She wouldn't see the doctor. She didn't want a man other than her husband near her. She hadn't let her husband see her naked body. Ever. The gray heads around me nodded and turned the invisible Wheel with a gentle movement of fingers in the space in front of their hearts.

They praised my cake and sipped my tea, drawing me into their circle, leaving me slices of rich history with the meat and vegetable dishes they brought.

There were things I didn't know: *Your daddy he no want no girl from Sixth Street. Your mama, she come from East some- place, come here teach children. He see her. He gonna have her, nobody else he want. Every girl this town sweet on your daddy. He could have any girl. But he want chuvar girl from*

44

East. *'Chuvar', you know that real America, no come from Old Country. Chew gum—chuvar, that what men call 'em they get off boat, see those American chew gum all time. Think pretty damn strange thing. Your daddy marry chuvar.* They stopped and shook their heads sadly in the sudden silence and crossed themselves.

There were pieces I knew already: *Your gramma, she come Sixth Street, no husband, six kids. She come here, she have no hair, just like man. We all think maybe something wrong with her. Sick. We find out she work in mine like man while husband dying. That back in Colorado. Mine foreman find out, big stink! She come Taylor no hair, but still she most beautiful woman! No husband. We think, oh boy! Then Mimi, Kiki come, eight kids now! Your gramma, she so poor, she work so hard, she do laundry for some people live above Main Street, feed kids saurkraut and just little tiny meat every night. She make little bit extra money, sell bootleg whisky. Buy shoes for kids. Then Eli come along, he want those jars your gramma use for whiskey. He want them for his wine he make, see. He marry her for those jars! He not so easy live with but take good care your gramma.* They contemplated Eli's many sins and few virtues. Some chuckled softly. They crossed themselves again, a blessing on his soul wherever it ended up.

And there was this that I learned about myself: *When your daddy move back home after your mamma she die, your grandma hold you all the time, sing to you. You just listen. She call you Mirna Mala. Quiet Little One. You only six months old, so tiny, but you never cry, you just listen her sing.*

I found that I, too, could add to this discussion. I did not have aches or pains, or secrets to tell, but I had stories, years of stories Gram had told me as we sat together on our couch, when something I had read to her or something we had heard on the radio sparked a memory. For years she murmured to the rhythm of Eli's snore, then later it was just her, her voice in the soft silence of our evening.

Did Gram ever tell you about the first time she walked down a street in America? I asked them.

No, they were all agreed, surprised even; she had never spoken about this.

Gram is just off the boat in New York.

My listeners nodded to each other murmured reverently, *Ellis Island.*

That's right. So, she decides she wants to see what an American city looks like. She takes a trolley and then walks around the streets a bit. She turns a corner, and here is this big glass shop window. In it are three men, all dressed up, very fancy, lying back in chairs with beautiful white towels over their faces. 'My God,' Gram thinks, ' what kind of place is this America? Dead bodies sitting in a store window like meat at a butcher's shop! What is this country I've come to?' she asks herself, and she starts to pray. She prays for herself and she prays for this poor godless country where they have no respect for the dead and especially she prays for these three dead men, that their souls will rise despite the embarrassment. Well, she's crossing herself and praying and crossing herself and suddenly, one of the dead men sits right up and pulls the beautiful white towel off his face! Then the guy next to him does the same thing! 'A miracle!' Gram thinks. She throws her hands up to heaven.

My listeners began to giggle. They shook their heads and mopped their eyes with their clutched hankies.

But then the barber comes up to the men and begins to paint their faces with cream...

I knew it! I knew those men no dead! announced Mrs. Kantar.

Oh, shush you! she is admonished by the others. They turned their attention back to me. *Go on, Mala.*

I was hearing Gram's laughter in theirs, her delight in a good joke on herself. *She always told me, she always said, 'Just for one minute I think I do big miracle...'*

We all smiled together. It was a good story, my first story.

Sitting with them, I saw these women's hands were never still. As they talked, they pointed and gestured. With words and wrinkled, roughened hands they wove into the air in front of them a silken garment, strong and binding, unseen but lovingly worn by all. Now my words were joined with theirs, their garment mine to wear. When an hour or two had passed, when the tea cups were empty and chill, the cake scattered crumbs, with a united sigh they pulled themselves up from chairs and couch and took their dishes to the kitchen. Against my protests they washed them with deft movements and left them to dry. At the front door, each gave me her blessing, a patted shoulder, a held hand, a touched cheek. Gathering their sweaters around them, they creaked out into the hot summer street.

We come back see you again, maybe couple days. Just check, maybe. ...Maybe bring you little something eat, they called back to me. It seemed I was joining the circle. Tea and cake with the widows...

Aunt Anna was never mentioned.

6

When Josie came home from work, she didn't even have a chance to kick off her high-heels or flop down into Eli's chair. I walked right up and put the present into her hands.

For me, Mala? she smiled, and standing right there by the front door, she pulled the ribbon loose and tore the paper.

She stared at the gift. Slippers. I had used red and yellow and blue yarn in nice wide stripes. The dingleballs on top had all three colors in them and were made especially large. For the space of time it took the wrapping paper to trace a fitful trail to the carpet, I wondered if she might drop them, turn around, and leave.

You knit? Her voice held as much enthusiasm as if she had heard that Aunt Anna was now moving in with us.

Gram taught me.

Ah.

The dingleballs are kind of large... I admitted.

My beloved dingleballs now looked sinister, as if they could devour the slender, dark hand that held them. The slippers' stripes seemed to glow and throb, lurid and over-bright. Josie raised her eyes from the slippers and blinked at me. I didn't know that look, what it meant, what she saw. We were two strangers, staring at each other in an unfamiliar room.

She took my hand and pulled me through the house, holding the slippers out in front of her and away from her body as if contagious.

I just thought... It's cold in the nights and mornings... I could...

In the kitchen I tried to redirect her attention.

Look. I made a cake! I said brightly. On the kitchen table a large chocolate sheet cake splayed beneath a weight of frosting the unfortunate color of Pepto Bismol. A little too much food coloring, I thought too late.

Sweet Jesus, Josie commented grimly and thrust me into her room. Still holding me, she closed the door and turned me around. I was confronted with myself in the full-length mirror on the back of her door.

I could make the dingleballs smaller... I look up hopefully into her reflection.

It's not the slippers, Mala, she said, and I had the slight satisfaction of knowing she had at least recognized them beneath the monstrous puffs of yarn that sat astride them.

Look at you, she said insistently. Compelled, I followed the line of her vision and looked at myself. Trussed-up in Gram's flowered apron, feet swimming in stretched-out house slippers, head anointed with cake flour, I was an awkward, unconvincing imposter.

You're thirteen, Mala. Thirteen-year-olds don't knit. They don't bake sheet cakes, and they sure as hell don't sit around gabbing with a bunch of old crows! You're becoming one of them, an honorary member of the widows' club! You should be doing stuff with friends, giggling over boys, getting into trouble, for God's sake! What are we going to do with you?

I put too much food coloring in the frosting. I know. Next time...

Josie was not listening. She was no longer seeing *me*.

Look at this hair, she muttered to herself. *No one under seventy-five wears her hair like this!*

I do, I yelped too late.

With quick, deft fingers she was pulling the hairpins from my braid, unwrapping the coil from my head, unbraiding thirteen years of ritual, every morning, first Gram's hair, then mine, the brushing, the braiding, wrapping the head, hiding the tattered end, securing the crown with pins. By the time I was ten, I could do it myself, and Gram could sit for the first time in her life, fussed over, every morning, like a queen. Josie ran long fingers through the kinked strands. My head tingled from the release.

Come on. She dragged me from the back room.

49

You don't like sheet cake. I don't have to make sheet cake!

Don't say another word, Mala, Josie warned.

She propelled me, silently, inexorably, in front of her, down the hall, into the bathroom. She turned on the taps in the sink and tested the water with her wrists, made slight adjustments and tested again.

I make a great nut bread, you know, povitza… Just like Gram.

That's it! she countered grimly and thrust my head under the warm, rushing water.

Josie added shampoo, hers, not Gram's, and worked up lather. Her hands worked my head as if it were my morning bread dough. She was creating. Awash in suds and water and Josie's determination, I clung to the sides of the basin as if I might be swept away and lost. She rinsed and squeezed the last of the water from my long hair and wrapped a towel around my head. She took me by the hand and led me, still sputtering, to the kitchen. She pulled out a chair and bowed me into it with a flourish, and then she unwrapped my head, leaving the towel around my shoulders to keep the dampness from my back. She fetched a comb and scissors and started in. The comb drew clean, deep furrows. She played with possible parts: center, right, settled for the left. She took up hunks of hair and used the old hairpins to hold them in loose loops against my head. A thin layer of hair was left to hang down. She began cutting, somewhere between chin and shoulder. My neck sensed the nearness of the cold metal blade, felt vulnerable, naked.

Did Gram ever tell you about Yuban?

Josie paused to consider, *Yuban? No.* She released a few pins, began cutting a new layer of hair.

Yuban was a blacksmith in her old village, in Yugoslavia. He was the most stubborn man in the village. And ornery, too. Mean as a devil, Gram said. One time, Yuban was shoeing a horse. But, this horse was just as mean as Yuban, and he didn't want to be shoed. Yuban had bent the old horse's front leg up and was crouched over its hoof pounding nails into the new shoe. Bam! Bam! Well, that horse just stretched its head back around and bit Yuban right on his fanny.

Josie stood still, scissors poised.

Yuban started swearing a blue streak and dropped the hammer and the hoof and stood up, looking that horse right in the eye the whole time. Then he walked around, behind the horse, and bit it right on its big, brown butt.

Josie grinned with satisfaction and began cutting again, releasing the last pins, swiftly finishing with strong, sure strokes.

The horse kicked Yuban so hard he flew in a giant arc out of the barn and into the yard. When he finally stood up he had to lean over and spit out teeth, all of them except two in the way back, on the top. He was never able to chew a piece of meat again the rest of his life.

Josie moved around in front of me. We stared at each other a long time, eyes narrowed.

Close, she ordered quietly and combed damp hair down over my face. She cut thin bangs in a neat line from temple to temple and gently brushed away the strands that clung to my nose, cheeks, and eyelashes. She used the towel to further dry and fluff my hair, then had me stand while she flicked the last of the hair from me. The long strands floated, glittering in the silent kitchen.

It just goes to show you, Josie said. *Pick your opponents wisely.* Her laughter was the sudden sound of wings, a flock of birds taking flight all at once.

You'll like this, Mala. Come see.

We went back to the mirror in her room. She placed her hands on my shoulders, possessive of her new creation.

Your hair's a beautiful color, Mala.

Pink.

What?

Gram called it pink. Pink hair.

She laughed again, a wheeling of joy through the air.

Gram had a limited vocabulary. It's strawberry blonde. It's the color of fire! There are actresses in Hollywood who would kill for that color!

She ran her fingers through it, separating the still-damp clumps, molding the ends into a pageboy, holding the weight of it up to my chin.

You're a new girl, Mala. She smiled down into my eyes. *You need a new name. Mala, what's that? It just means 'little one' in Serb.* She was holding my head now, checking its size and shape. *I don't even know your name!* she laughed, and gave my head a slight shake.

Rebecca.

In my mind I was hearing *Rebecca Jean Talovich.* It was the first day of every school year. *Rebecca Jean Talovich?* The teachers lived above Main, in houses the colors of Easter eggs. They always looked through the back rows for this Talovich girl, the back rows with their dark glossy heads and bright brown eyes. *Rebecca Jean Talovich?* They skipped over the pink-haired one in that sea of brown. I wanted to correct the teacher, tell her I was not Rebecca Jean Talovich, the pale, pink, and white American girl standing in front of her, unnoticed, a pastel mint left untouched in a china dish. I was Mala Talovich, a dark, fierce Serb. *Rebecca Jean Talovich!?* I raised my arm. *Oh, there you are. Speak up next time, dear. Nickolas Udopolous?* Someone always told her later. *Everybody calls her Mala,* they said. The teacher would focus on me, weak blue eyes behind thick lenses. *Why?*

Becky. It's perfect! Josie hugged me as if she was greeting a long lost relative. *Let's clean up all that hair, Becky,* she added.

We swept the hair into a soft mound of shining gold.

You know, Josie said, considering the pile, *sometimes the birds have a second clutch of eggs in the summer. We should scatter all this outside. I bet the birds would love all this for their nests. Won't those eggs be happy!*

She gathered the hair and carried it to the back door. She lifted her arms and spread her hands and the hair drifted down and out into the cool evening. All through the rest of the night, Josie glowed, warming me with her attention. She wore the slippers. We ate cake, and she told me about what she thought college would be like.

You'll be ready to take on this whole town, she said, adding gently, *when I leave.*

Leave. The word floated in the air in front of me, then sank slowly under its own weight. Josie reached over to run her fingers through my hair, fluff my bangs, train a strand behind my ear. She was pleased with her work. She had peeled back the stubborn shell and let loose a bright, new chick. Birth is a matter of timing.

The next morning, I woke up early to make bread. With the sun not quite over the cliffs above town, I kneaded dough in the blue air. I wore Gram's apron, a new name, and new hair, hair that the actresses in Hollywood would kill for. In the quiet kitchen, I planned my day. I would sit in a circle of old women and listen. Perhaps I would tell them about my hair and the actresses in Hollywood. They would like that. In the afternoon, I would call some of my cousins and Carrie Price, my best friend and motherless like me. Maybe we'd go watch a ballgame up at the park. Then we'd come back for cards when the wind kicked up. I'd let them stay until Josie came home. She could kick them out. She'd like that.

Out in the back yard, the birds fluttered and squabbled, gathering each strand of hair until the ground was bare. They lined their nests with gold to warm temporary children. With a flash of wings, the children would rise, soar, leave.

Part 2

7

Gram's was just the first death of the summer, important to our family, something to contemplate and sadden Sixth Street, of little notice to the town at large. Three weeks after Gram's funeral, just as Josie and I had settled into a rhythm of life together, a death occurred that drew in the entire town. William Pete had been sheriff in Taylor for five years before Gram had shown up. The Copper King mining company had hired him out of a small farming town in Utah that seemed unusually glad to be rid of him. He was a bachelor and could trace his heritage back to one of Brigham Young's forty wives, so the company thought it was getting a bargain. It didn't have to pay him enough to feed a family, but he would be a clean-living Mormon. *American,* the managers at the smelter all nodded in agreement. They didn't know that William Pete was a Jack Mormon. At an early age, he had fallen off the religious bandwagon. In truth, there wasn't a vice that he didn't savor, practice openly, and enthusiastically recommend to anyone who'd listen. The move from Utah to Nevada suited him as well as it suited the little town he was leaving. Nevada had possibilities. So did William Pete. He turned out to be a great sheriff. He kept the uneasy peace in a town where cultures, religions, and generations sought but refused to yield understanding. Sheriff Billy looked after the people in Taylor with a mixture of gentle diplomacy and whiskey, turned a blind eye to most of the shenanigans, and was genuinely sorry when he had to jail someone. Once you were in his cell, you became his personal drinking partner and the perfect opponent in endless, low-stakes games of blackjack and poker. He cheated with relish, and from behind his set of bars you were in no position to complain. If you were sent to the State Pen for your crime, he gallantly waved the gambling debt you had accrued. Should you be found innocent, you were sent home with a bill that could reach into the hundreds of dollars. Sheriff Billy always collected. Other than crimes of passion, Taylor became a law-abiding town. We couldn't afford otherwise.

Gram and Sheriff Billy had been friends and business partners. When Gram came to town toting six children and one trunk of belongings she was dead broke. Migrating west after she'd buried her husband, Taylor was as far as the money went. She and the children sat in a line on their trunk at the one-window station while the dust rose in the northwest and then barreled over them. They huddled against it, each wondering, *What is this place?* Later, the sun set in jeweled tones in a pale, clean sky. Just before nightfall, a red-faced man with a paunch and the uneven gait of a man considerably inebriated approached. He wore a cowboy hat and a star on his Levi jacket. Gram and her children spent the night in a jail cell. He left the cell door wide open so she'd understand she wasn't being arrested. There was a hot meal from somewhere, bacon, eggs scrambled with fried onions. While the children took turns swinging on the open cell door, Sheriff Billy slowly explained the basics of poker to my weary, uncomprehending grandmother. She gambled twenty dollars she didn't have and with a shaking hand signed a note she couldn't read. But by the time she and the children awoke the next morning, Sheriff Billy had arranged for a house down on Sixth Street, down where *her people* lived, and a few laundry jobs to keep her going. It took him three years to collect his twenty dollars. When it became obvious that laundry wasn't going to feed Gram's growing family, Sheriff Billy arranged for her to supplement her income by selling bootleg whiskey. He loaned Gram the money to buy Ball jars. Then, glowing like a furnace and gasping for every breath, he hiked up into the mountains behind town with my dad and my uncles Sam and Mike to introduce his very young business partners to his favorite distiller. Once a week, the boys were to carry down buckets of bootleg whiskey for their mom to bottle up and sell. Gram only handed out a second Ball jar when the first was returned. Customers paid for any breakage. She had the law behind her, so her business was brisk and well behaved. Sheriff Billy showed up at Gram's front door on Mondays, Wednesdays, and Saturdays at 4:00 p.m., just after the dust had settled. In his quiet, reasonable way, he'd say he'd heard that she might be selling liquor without a state license.

Oh no, Sheriff Beely, Gram would say. *I no sell no booze. I have maybe just little bit here, give to my friends. You come in taste little bit. You see. This no good stuff. Nobody buy this booze. You come taste!*

Sheriff Billy spent the next two hours at Gram's kitchen table, having something to eat and making sure the whiskey was not worth selling. It was a lucrative business for both. Sheriff Billy obligingly took his profits in trade. When the favorite distiller died in a tragic but not unexpected explosion, Sheriff Billy decided that Gram needed a permanent solution to her financial woes. She needed a husband. It was Sheriff Billy who pointed Eli Milivich, a Serb miner living in the company's bachelor quarters, in the direction of Gram and her Ball jars. Eli made wine, good wine. Sheriff Billy had sampled it quite often, had even won a gallon jug off of Eli once when Eli had spent a night in jail after a drunken brawl. Gram had empty Ball jars. Eli had wine. Eli had a steady job. Gram had eight kids. Eli presented his case. Gram shrugged and nodded consent. After a business-like civil service, Eli moved in. For the next twenty-five years, Gram fed him, did his laundry, put up with his nasty temper and, finally, missed him when he died. All during Eli's tenure in Gram's house, Sheriff Billy still came. After a big plate of something good, the two men sat in kitchen chairs on the front porch—weather permitting—comparing vintages, smoking cigars, swapping stories, and watching the town pass by.

Sheriff Billy's town.

More than liquor, more than fat, evil-smelling cigars, more than eggs, bacon and fried onions, more even than gambling and always winning, Sheriff Billy loved the prostitutes over in Parker. His favorite spot was a joint called The Yum-Yum Tree. The faded sign on the front of the old wooden, two-storied shack showed a tree trunk sprouting female legs, splayed and naked except for spike-heeled shoes in assorted colors. Although he patronized all three whorehouses with equal cheer, it was the fruit of The Yum-Yum Tree that Sheriff Billy savored the most. The women there were athletic. They matched him in enthusiasm, but surpassed him in health and youth, a combination that was bound to catch up with Sheriff Billy one day. The day was a Tuesday, June 26th, 1:15 in the afternoon.

When the bouncer of the Yum-Yum Tree, Harold Deen, heard Dolores scream, he thought, *What the hell are they getting up to now?* He shrugged and went back to his sports page. When the second scream came, he dropped the paper and took the rickety stairs two at a time, shaking the entire building in his effort to reach Dolores' room. He stopped short at the closed door. He knew Sheriff Billy was inside, and Harold was perplexed as to what to do. A small crowd of ladies gathered around him in the narrow hall. The door whipped open and Dolores screamed a third time right into Harold's huge chest.

What the hell, Dolores? Harold bellowed down at her.

Dolores could only point. Through the door, the colossal mound of Sheriff Billy's naked stomach could be seen on the bed. He wasn't moving. Dolores, Harold, and the other ladies crowded into the tiny room. It was functional and stark; a sink and towel rack hung from one wall, a wooden chair and single metal cot pressed the opposite wall. The largest thing in the room was Sheriff Billy, a whale beached on the narrow white shelf of Dolores' bed. His eyes were open and staring; a huge grin was solidifying on his face. There was no doubt about two things: Sheriff Billy was happy, and he was dead.

Jesus, Dolores. What did you do? Harold whispered in awe.

The usual! Dolores wailed.

The other prostitutes closed around her like a protective phalanx. Some discussion ensued. Should they try to dress Sheriff Billy, carry his huge bulk downstairs and prop him in a corner of the couch, maybe place a movie magazine in his lap? They tested the theory amongst themselves. *He was sitting there looking at Betty Grable, officer. It was just too much for his heart.* It didn't ring true. It didn't seem right. Staring down at the jubilant face of Sheriff Billy, Harold and the whores experienced Truth: this was just the way Sheriff Billy was meant to go, and he'd want everyone to know it, too. So they didn't touch Sheriff Billy. Harold Deen went downstairs to call the Parker police and the women arranged themselves around their favorite customer like mourning angels marking the passing of a great man. When the police and the coroner arrived, they asked Dolores to be a bit more specific as to the particulars of 'the usual.' The men eyed the grinning Sheriff Billy, clearly impressed. Despite her misery over killing Sheriff Billy, she foresaw a time of increased prosperity ahead that allowed Dolores to smile tearfully up at the circle of uniforms and at the speculative coroner in his white smock.

Sheriff Billy seemed to have expanded since he entered Dolores' room. He had gained at least a hundred pounds of satisfaction. It was an almost impossible task to heave his body from the cot. Inching him through Dolores' narrow door was a feat of engineering that took Harold Deen, the whole police force, most of the prostitutes, and two unsuspecting customers who arrived just in time to see Sheriff Billy's grinning face and naked body make a sideways entrance into the hall and then stop there, hopelessly wedged. The coroner waited in his station wagon out front, tapping the wheels and checking his watch. He wanted to have the postmortem over. He was making plans for the evening. *Dolores, Dolores,* he sighed.

When news of Sheriff Billy's death reached Taylor, the reactions were mixed. Sheriff Billy's rule had been a long and peaceful one, but it was not without critics. Above Main Street, the mostly *chuvar* population was relieved that this eyesore of a man, this lover of liquor and cigars, rich food and willing women, this reprobate behind a badge was finally gone. They didn't pray for Sheriff Billy's soul; contrary to doctrine, some things were beyond redemption. Farther up the hill still, in the offices of the smelter, a handful of men in suits worried. Layoffs had been scheduled in two weeks time. The price of copper was dropping, and production was moving to other, cheaper countries. Sheriff Billy would not be there to soothe the angry miners and smelter workers with cajoling words and free whiskey. The company could not have guessed all those years ago that the man they picked as sheriff for their little empire would dole out justice and manage the mixed populace in such a unique and fitting way. It had been happenstance, not likely to be repeated. There would never be another Sheriff Billy. The company quietly began a search for a man who could do the job—if not with gentle words, then with a strong arm.

On Sixth Street, we heard the news with a mixture of sadness and amusement. The old women shook their heads and crossed themselves. The Holy Wheel had rolled right over their Sheriff Billy. Without a word, dark, little eyes in wrinkled faces twinkled this shared message: *Good way die! Sheriff Beely smiling in Heaven now maybe.*

In the basement of the hospital, the coroner had finished his autopsy. Cutting through layers of what Sheriff Billy had happily called 'hibernation insurance,' the coroner had found signs of a massive coronary in a dangerously enlarged heart.

Taylor's undertaker, Udiah Simple, had come to take the body away. An argument had ensued. The coroner wanted to leave the grin on Sheriff Billy's face.

It's an affront to God! hollered Undertaker Simple. *It's against the Book. Jesus and all the Latter Day Saints are watching!*

I don't care who the hell is watching, Udiah. Sheriff

William Pete died smiling. With good reason, I might add. The coroner allowed himself a small sigh of appreciation. *How often does a man die smiling? I say let him go to the grave with it!*

The two men stared at each other for a time over the still mound of Sheriff Billy. Finally, the undertaker put on his hat, adjusted the peak and the brim, and left without either the body or another word. The coroner answered Sheriff Billy's grin with a wide, satisfied one of his own.

Behind the wheel of his hearse, Udiah Simple was smiling, too, reminding himself that there was more that one battle in a holy war. Once he had Sheriff William Pete in the back room of his funeral parlor, he could do pretty much whatever he wanted.

News of the argument traveled through town at a brisk pace. At the Taylor Club, bets were taken. Would Sheriff Billy smile? The tallies were dead even. The light of heart and the optimistic showed the color of their money, nodding yes, absolutely; the sheriff would smile. The cynical shook their heads sadly at their benighted comrades. They punched a thumb over their shoulders, pointing across Main Street, at the orderly town that stretched up the hillside toward the smelter and the smokestack and the dark boundary of the cliffs. It would never happen. Sheriff Billy would be planted like any other corpse—stern, sour, and sad. On the hillside, in quiet houses on paved streets, pale-haired wives sipped mint tea, exchanging sainted smiles. They didn't condone gambling, but they knew a thing or two. They knew Udiah Simple. They knew that the righteous prevail.

Perhaps Sheriff Billy may have started out a descendent of Brigham, but he had slipped from that lofty locale. A church service was out of the question. The question of sin aside, the Catholic priest and the Baptist minister from Parker felt uncomfortable burying a Mormon. The Mormons wouldn't bury him at all. For a short time it seemed that there would be no clergy to preside over Sheriff Billy's body, and he would be sent off by a curious throng of friends and foes without anybody to stand by the graveside and utter those few, carefully chosen words that applied to the dead man. Then, the Methodist-Minister-Without-A-Flock stepped forward. A free agent, the Methodist-Minister-Without-A-Flock was also a man to whom sin was not a stranger. He looked kindly on the foibles of other men. In fact, he and Sheriff Billy had spent many evenings at the jail, gambling until dawn. At the time of Sheriff Billy's death, the Methodist-Minister-Without-A-Flock had owed him $4,262. Because the minister had no job, and thereby no means of paying, the sheriff obligingly extended unlimited credit. Sheriff Billy was patient; some day, he figured, Methodists were bound to move to Taylor. He died waiting for the payoff. On his side, the minister thought providing a rousing sermon and a heart-felt farewell would close the account nicely. Unaware, the residents of Sixth Street collected money to pay for his services.

Oh no, the Methodist-Minister-Without-A-Flock said in his most sonorous voice. *This is a duty I would gladly do for nothing...*

Well, he amended quickly. *Maybe just a few dollars. Things are a bit tight at the moment.* Somewhere in the back of his mind, slot machines jangled softly.

By the time of the burial, Udiah Simple had had Sheriff Billy's body in his care for two days. During that time he had collected the sheriff's tan uniform from the Yum-Yum Tree where it had been left on a chair in Dolores' room and forgotten in the excitement of the sheriff's departure. Udiah Simple stood three paces back from the front door and leaned way forward to knock. He leaned back and waited, his nose wrinkled. He was sure he could detect the whiff of sin, cheap perfume, booze and heated bodies oozing from the cracks around the loose-fitting door. He took an extra step back. From above, the prostitutes giggled down through the window at the black-clad undertaker. They considered dropping Sheriff Billy's boots and uniform on Simple's head, but they had lovingly washed and pressed the worn old uniform and polished the old boots and didn't want to undo their labor. Dolores eventually delivered the uniform to the door, wearing a black lace bra of remarkably diminutive dimensions and gossamer half-slip with nothing on underneath, an outfit she had changed into for the undertaker's particular benefit.

Be careful with these, Undertaker, Dolores said in her smokiest voice. Udiah Simple hissed and snatched at the clothes, sweat breaking out at his hairline.

Come back and see me again! Dolores yoo-hooed and waved from the open doorway as the hearse spit gravel and tore down the road.

Safely back in the prep room of the funeral home, Udiah Simple, still overheated from his encounter with the ripened peach of the Yum-Yum tree, set to work with shaking fingers. The first thing he did was to wipe the smile off Sheriff Billy's face. This calmed Udiah enormously, and he continued with renewed professionalism. With cool efficiency, Sheriff Billy was embalmed, his toenails and fingernails cleaned and cut off in even square lines, his thin gray hair washed, trimmed, parted on the wrong side, and the curls combed out and held down with a shellac of Brillcream. Udiah Simple dressed Sheriff Billy's body, rolled clean socks onto the cold feet, and pulled the gleaming old boots on. He added a few touches of powder and rouge to Sheriff Billy's face, a hint of red to his lips, and then, cranking the gurney up with a foot pedal, he angled its metal surface down and slid the now ready body into its casket. As a final touch, he placed Sheriff Billy's cowboy hat on his chest and crossed his hands up over the crown. Udiah Simple stood back to admire his work.

The undertaker was not completely satisfied. It seemed to him that a hint of smirk hovered around Sheriff Billy's lips, the half-remembered tug of some stubborn muscle. Udiah Simple paced a few steps and looked from another angle.

Surely not, he thought to himself. He strode up close to the casket and thrust his face down toward Billy's.

Surely not... he whispered to Sheriff Billy and traced the line of his lips with a light touch.

Sheriff Billy seemed to emit a chemical sigh. Powder found its way to Udiah Simple's nose.

Surely Not, said Udiah with loud authority to the empty room. Rearing back, reaching up and then down, he closed the lid on Sheriff Billy's coffin with a sharp finality.

On the widely anticipated morning of Sheriff Billy's send off, it was hot by 8:00 a.m.. The sun sapped the blue from the sky, torched the streets of Taylor. Udiah Simple wheeled Sheriff Billy's coffin from the back room in the funeral home and out into the middle of the front parlor. He opened the double doors, hoping to catch any slight breeze and clear the taint in the air. The sun from the windows caught the coffin lid and shot sparks of light off the lacquered oak. A long line of towns-people was forming at the front door. The clock inched forward. For a moment, Udiah Simple watched the crowd as it stood in the baking sun, enjoying its size and the building feeling of anticipation that begged admittance through his doors. Men stood fanning themselves with Fedoras, and women angled hands against the sun to shade their eyes or pulled black shawls protectively over gray heads. Udiah checked his watch. 9:00 a.m. exactly. He stepped forward, smiling.

The crowd surged. Udiah Simple led the flock in to the waiting coffin. The parlor was quickly filled, the line still spilling onto the porch, down the steps, and into the street. Udiah moved to the head of the coffin. With a flourish of utter confidence tingeing his usual black-clad dignity, Udiah Simple swung open the lid. A mixed gasp and cheer rose from the assemblage. The sound rippled out the double doors, gathered strength and volume on the porch, and then, rolled along the white-hot street. Money began changing hands.

The sun poured in, bathing Sheriff Billy's face. Udiah Simple's smile faltered, was eclipsed, by Billy's, who lay in the powerful light of day, grinning his last laugh.

8

I hitched a ride to the cemetery with Aunt Anna and Uncle Nick. Once there, I found a knot of cousins and friends who had inched into front row spots. I wedged myself between my best friend Carrie Price and my cousin Paul. The sharp edge of the grave dropped away into darkness six inches from our toes. The casket hung just above the hole, waiting to be lowered. Behind us the crowd pressed and murmured. At the head of the casket, the Methodist-Minister-Without-a-Flock cleared his throat, folded his hands, and began.

Friends...friends, we are here to say goodbye to Sheriff William Pete. Our Sheriff Billy. He was a good man...

The Methodist-Minister-Without-a-Flock hesitated; the crowd leaned forward, worried.

...and a good poker player.

The crowd exhaled and sat back on their heels.

...He was a man who never lost. He had remarkable luck...I'd say...

The crowd shifted uncomfortably in their dark clothes and memories. Shoulders rubbed; collars tightened and scratched; hot moisture gathered in folds of flesh.

...In life, friends...in life, we are dealt only one hand. We can only guess whether to stand pat or fold... Should we draw to an inside straight? What about a possible full house? What are the wild cards? Who decides? How much should you risk that that next card's gonna give you a flush? Just how much should you risk? It's a beautiful... No! A terrible mystery!

The Methodist-Minister-Without-a-Flock's voice deepened, filled with exalted knowledge, and rolled out across Sheriff Billy's casket.

Friends...friends! He reached out to us.

Sometimes, sometimes we just want to pull that queen right off the discard pile! That's right! Take it back!

His voice lowered to a hoarse whisper of despair.

But we can't...

I felt a sharp elbow in my side. My cousin Paul rolled his eyes. Carrie leaned around the front of me to catch his attention. Her violet eyes crinkled at the corners, her black curls bounced and hung suspended for just a moment, midair over the coffin. She flashed a grin of perfect white teeth, a deep dimple drilled into her left cheek. Paul flushed and grinned back. Tall and grave in his limp suit, Dr. Price glanced across the coffin at his daughter, Carrie, then dropped his eyes to study his brown oxfords. I could feel Aunt Anna's eyes silently boring into our heads from a few rows back.

Friends! LIFE IS A CRAP SHOOT!

The Methodist-Minister-Without-a-Flock raised one fist to heaven and shook it wildly. His arm swept downward. His fist opened. We watched, mesmerized by the path of invisible dice as they rolled off his fingers. We could hear them clatter over Sheriff Billy's casket and come to rest at the spot where Sheriff Billy's boots pointed skyward under the lid.

Snake Eyes!

The crowd jumped.

*Luck is a funny thing...*the Methodist-Minister-Without-a-Flock whispered, nodding.

Luck is indeed a funny thing...

The Methodist-Minister-Without-a-Flock's eulogy washed through the crowd. He maneuvered smoothly from craps to roulette, had begun on twenty-one and was wrestling with the intricacies of doubling down when a line of five cars rolled sedately up the hill of the cemetery. The Methodist-Minister-Without-a-Flock stood with his mouth open, his concentration broken, his inspiration fled. In the gap of sudden silence we watched the approaching procession.

Dust rose no higher than the cars' fenders, but the drivers waited behind the steering wheels of their cars until the air had settled into quiet expectation. From each car an unfamiliar man emerged, ignoring the gaping crowd, and walked around the car, opening doors in the blazing silence. At first we didn't recognize these men in their crisp dark suits and felt fedoras. As their first passenger emerged, it became obvious: a high-heeled shoe, a lean ankle in a pale silk stocking, a knee not hastily covered. Every prostitute in Parker, sixteen of them, escorted by their narrow barmen and muscled bouncers, had come to pay Sheriff Billy their respects. The women wore wide-brimmed hats to shade their makeup. The sun shimmered off the rich material of their dresses and winked from the golden snaps on their handbags. Their white gloves glowed. Walking toward the grave, they moved in a perfumed breeze of their own making. Their clothing whispered. Around the grave, the crowd parted and gave way. They clustered by the side of Sheriff Billy's casket, swaying slightly in their too-high heels, a bouquet of exotic blooms on slender stems. Their men edged them protectively. From mid-air the birds marveled at the transformed landscape and wondered where to land.

The Methodist-Minister-Without-a-Flock cleared his throat, then cleared his throat again.

*Friends...*he said tentatively into the thick, hot air. *Sheriff Billy was a good man. He was a good man and a good poker player.*

Back on familiar ground, we sighed. The Methodist-Minister-Without-a-Flock struggled to move forward. His voice floated in the quiet, perfumed heat, a cork in an eddy. Our attention wavered and dissipated.

Sheriff William Pete was dealt a good hand...

The Minister's voice had ebbed to a murmur.

...but it didn't have staying power...

One of the prostitutes leaned over to whisper something into another's ear, their hats trembling in collusion.

...He was forced to fold too early in the game...

Two magpies lit on the power line by the highway. Their black and white wings stroked the air, reaching for balance on the swaying wire. Still smiling, the prostitute who had just whispered raised her head to watch the birds.

...His luck ran out...

The sun washed across her face.

...William Pete was my friend, the Minister said simply.

But no one was listening. We were transfixed by a radiant face, a smile of perfect white teeth, a dimple deep in a left cheek, a set of violet eyes crinkling merrily at the corners. She raised a gloved hand to rearrange a glossy black curl. A gasp and then a soft sibilancy swept from the edges of the grave.

I will miss him...

The Methodist-Minister-Without-a-Flock bent his head.

Let us pray...

Heads dropped with practiced response, but every eye watched the tight triangle suddenly formed over the casket: the man, the beautiful prostitute, and Carrie. From the back came a murmur of protest and some tried to muscle forward, heads still dutifully bent. Carrie clung to my arm, staring at the woman. The crowd inched us forward toward the open grave. Her head swiveled from the woman to her father and stayed there, watching. He, too, was looking at the woman. There was no surprise in his face, just a painful openness, as if the sight of her had scrubbed him clean of all the gravity and patience and defeat that normally protected him. Sun was suddenly bright in his face, and he blinked. The sharp line of his jaw softened and trembled. One hand crept forward from his side, two inches, three, as if he might reach over Sheriff Billy's body to the woman. He swallowed and dropped his hand, glanced at Carrie, but she had turned away. From the prostitute there was no response, no hint of recognition, nothing. The hat dipped, the beautiful face was obscured. She shimmered and wavered like a mirage at the edge of the grave, contemplating Sheriff Billy's casket as it was slowly eased into the ground.

Amen! roared The Methodist-Minister-Without-a-Flock.

As dirt sounded on the lid of the casket, the prostitutes

drifted like petals back to their cars, their escorts moving purposefully ahead to open doors and hand them in. The snap of the car doors was enormous and startling in the vacuum of their leaving. The cars crunched sedately down the hill and out on the highway, back towards Parker and business as usual. We were once again monochrome, yet utterly changed by the encounter. Uncomfortable, the mourners shuffled and mumbled and settled themselves into familiar groupings, seeking comfort in the fevered landscape. Our eyes betrayed us. Some could not quite look at the doctor still standing caught at the edge of the grave. Others could not look away. So they complained quietly of the heat and the dirt and headed for home. Only the sexton with his shovel, the doctor, and Carrie remained, markers beneath the punishing sky. Around them air stirred. Off on the other side of The Sands the crisp edges of the world flowed and dust began to rise.

In her car, Aunt Anna whistled low. She fired the engine until it whined in complaint, and then punched the car into gear. We rocketed down the rutted cemetery road. Uncle Nick clung to the passenger seat with both hands; Paul, Sofie, and I ricocheted painfully against the armrests and each other in the back seat. With a thump we hit the final rut at the entrance to the highway and leapt onto the backtop. Aunt Anna didn't even check for traffic. The ride became unnaturally smooth and quiet.

Holy Mother of God, Aunt Anna exhaled into the dusty air of the car. *Did you see that?*

See what? Uncle Nick asked.

The doctor, that whore? Aunt Anna was looking at Uncle Nick incredulously.

He was rubbing his head where it had hit the roof of the car. Perhaps he attended a different funeral.

I was listening to the Minister-Without-a-Flock, Uncle Nick said defensively, then added hopefully, *It was a nice sermon.*

Aunt Anna stared hard at Uncle Nick. She reached over

and smacked him. He jumped. His head banged the roof again.

Anna! Ow!

Aunt Anna shook her head and stomped on the gas.

Paul, Sofie, and I sat quiet and awed in the back seat. We struggled with vision and meaning: the man, the woman, our friend Carrie. Carrie trembling at the graveside, suddenly reduced, the product of an inexplicable equation.

I thought about luck.

The Methodist-Minister-Without-a-Flock was right. Everything in life could turn in an instant. The dip of a black and white wing, the tilt of a head, a hand held out. These were portents. You have to be watchful. You have to read the sky and sniff the wind. Otherwise, you might miss the small connections that add up to meaning. You might fold too early or not at all. You might end up losing everything.

9

That night I dreamed of my own mother.

I followed her as she walked through the town in a pale gray dress and low, slip-on shoes. She crossed Main Street near the ballpark. I heard the intermittent crack of bat on ball, cheers and shouts from the bleachers. She never turned her head. She threaded her soundless way through the streets of upper town, past yards with sprinklers where children shrieked and ran through icy droplets. She walked beneath tall cottonwoods. Though their roots erupted through the sidewalk and made walking difficult, she never stumbled, her passage from this place so smooth and sure. At the top of town she followed the fence around the smelter and then cut behind the smokestack. She was following the trail the bootlegger used twenty years before. It angled up through waist-high sagebrush and tumbleweeds to the base of the cliffs and cut a jagged path up the mountain through outcroppings of limestone and across precarious slides of loose dirt and pebble. She never hesitated. She knew each handhold, each spot for her light-soled shoes, each root or square inch of firm ground or stone that would hold her weight.

Suddenly on top, she stood in empty, blue sky. A thousand feet below, the little town in its gray valley was another world, a patch of minor movement and intent. The wind gathered her skirt and lifted it. Sunset-lit, she floated, clean, untouchable, feet resting on air. Just below the lip of the ridge I had reached the extent of my tether. I could not seem to gain the top with her. The turbulent life of Taylor washed up the mountain toward us: the distant crowd at the ballpark, mothers calling children in to dinner, the six o'clock whistle, the sound of boots on hard ground and laughter as the men left the day shift at the smelter and headed down the streets toward home. The good smell of a hundred suppers swept up from the town on the cooling air. Just-baked bread (Gram's bread?) scented the cliff face as I clung there. But these ghosts of Taylor could not reach the woman on the ridge either. Caught by the breeze that buoyed her, the smells and sounds of Taylor came apart and disappeared. Her back was to town. She looked out east. I could not see what she saw. She was a slender shadow against the darkening sky.

It was that first step that undid her, a slight hesitation, an instant of vertigo as she turned and the valley tipped up to catch her. I wished to replay that moment, watch for meaning, for decision or mistake.

The rest of her journey was flight. Nothing impeded her progress through night air. Bone-shattering rock and cold earth waited to absorb her. I fell too, silently, forever, coming to rest inside her, arms splayed, legs bent under, staring through sightless eyes up from the crook of the mountain where cliff meets valley floor. The night sky revolved above us slowly, the distance between stars deep, infinite.

The early whistle blew. On cue, the sky turned pearly above us. The town stirred. Slammed doors, echoed laughter, cars, bacon, radio music, feet on the hill toward work... The waking town tugged me gently from my resting place, gathered me into textures of life and drew me home to Gram's house. A baby I knew slept there unaware, securely swaddled in the middle of a double bed. Rolls of soft blankets keeping her safe from the edge.

It was the start of a day like any day, every day. The town breathed out and in, settling in the rhythm of living. The woman lying against the bosom of the cliff went unnoticed, unsought for some time. Then eventually unremembered.

But I had spent a night with her. We had covered rough terrain. We had hurtled toward earth, like a hawk toward its intention. Like a meteor. We had lain silent under the wheel of the sky and measured the heavens.

10

In the days that followed Sheriff Billy's funeral heat waves pulsed above the dusty streets, buoying rumors that drifted on their own currents through the town. Every citizen in Taylor discussed Doctor Price and the prostitute and the child, my friend Carrie, who lived with the one and was the spitting image of the other. Down on Sixth Street the coven of old women gathered in my front room. With their offerings and invocations they turned the Holy Wheel, nodded, and spun truths from the dust motes in the dim air behind my drawn curtains. To them, he had always been *poor doctor.*

...I go see poor doctor for my feet...

...Poor doctor give me medicine for back...

It was not his hard work, long hours, or low pay that made him a poor man. It was his constant, tired kindness, the defeated slant of his thin shoulders, the gaunt, sad face. These women, schooled in life, recognized hunger in all its forms.

That poor doctor, he need woman. Take care him and little girl.

Well, it seemed he'd had a woman, once.

No good woman...

Better no woman.

The doctor's fate was sealed with a slow shaking of gray heads, a sign of the Cross. All was explained, accepted, forgiven with a gentle waving of crooked, old fingers.

Josie, who had missed the funeral because of work, wanted every detail from me.

Well, well, well, Dr. Price, she said with delight.

Her sentiment was generally shared by the younger wives and women along Sixth Street. They had inherited from their mothers a certain amused attachment to the antics of men. Above Main, women sat around kitchen tables doing mental math and comparing notes.

...That little girl's thirteen...

...The doctor's been here, what, six-seven years?

...How long's that woman been up at The Green Willow?

...Years...

...Do you think he knew?

They shuddered delicately.

...They say she's known as The Divine...

...Famous...

...Men come from as far as Elko...

It was suddenly discovered that Dr. Price had an uncanny resemblance to a young Boris Karloff.

...It's those eyes...

...those long bony hands...

...skinny neck...

...the very same cowlick!

They shivered in unison.

As a town we were addicted to horror films and screwball comedies. Drama bored us. Depending on point of view and geographic location, the women of Taylor were recasting poor Dr. Price as the sinister madman, the tortured monster, or the unlikely hero of a surprising farce. On one thing, however, they were all agreed. There was only one reason why the situation had gone undetected.

Men!

If it had been women sneaking that thirty miles to Parker Saturday night...

Why, we would have known ages ago!

Men don't notice a thing unless it comes up and slaps them across the face!

I'd like to slap some faces!

Men!

For their part, the men of Taylor were keeping a low profile. They couldn't quite figure it out, but they had been judged guilty of something. In the Pool Hall and the Taylor Club, they winked at each other and grinned into their beers.

Others were indeed feeling slapped, but not by their wives. They were having a hard time meeting Doc Price's eye when he passed them in the searing street. Their eyes followed the retreating figure, though, watching the gentle swing of the black bag, the gaunt shoulders, the bowed head, until at last he disappeared around a corner or into a house. *Divine*, they whispered to themselves, tasting the word and then shaking their heads in wonder. How? It was the question in everyone's mind.

Curiosity burned at a fever pitch. Strange, unrelated symptoms emerged, a back ache on J Street, unbearably itchy skin two streets over, sudden blurred vision, a cough coming on, an old war wound acting up on K Street, on upper Main rickets. There was a general, urgent need for medical attention in nearly every family. Carrie called to report on the epidemic.

You should see Dad's clinic. It's jammed. Everyone sitting around with their fake aches and pains, dying for a chance to gawk at him, see if he says anything...

Has he said anything?

Sure. 'You need some rest, Mrs. Pastervich.' 'Better cut down on the roughage, Mrs. Deen.'

She had perfected the soft, tired cadence, the slight pause of each weighed word.

Not to them, Carrie. To you.

Silence on the line.

Not much, she sighed and paused again, this time with an unconscious echoing of her father's speech, testing the weight of words.

I asked him if her knew her. He said yes, a long time ago. I asked him who she was. He said it was pretty obvious what she is. I said that she looked kind of like me. He said yes. Then I just blurted it out. I couldn't help it. 'Is she my mother?' I asked. He shook his head and said, 'Carrie, does she seem like the kind of person who could be a mother?' Then he walked out the door. He had house calls to make.

I don't get it, I worried. *What does that mean?*

Silence stretched along the copper line.

I don't know.

In my mind, I had a sudden clear image: a woman on a high, rocky cliff, dark sky behind her, far beneath her feet a waiting, gray town. It was the moment before flight.

It's important to know. If you can...

Yes.

So what are you going to do?

I don't know yet. Something. I'll tell you one thing. I'm not leaving this house until people around here find something else to whisper about.

Well...anyway...let me know...

I will. Bye.

Bye.

The phone was dead before I could add, *Good luck, Carrie.*

From clear across town I could feel the silence in Carrie's house, could see her sitting behind closed blinds, alone, while her dad doggedly attended the patients at his clinic and made house calls. All the wonder, horror, wild speculation flying around town was distilled and purified in this one, solitary girl. She would work things out for herself like she always did. When she had gathered her questions, devised her plan of inquiry, she would call. Like me, there were things she now needed to know.

As I waited for her call, I followed the ghost of my own mother. I tried to patch together a picture of her from what words I could remember. There was almost nothing left beyond to mark her journey through this place. There was no grave to stand over, to bring flowers to, or to watch slowly age. When she died, her body was shipped out on an east-bound train. Her parents wanted her to be buried with her family. Her Family. Her personal items were put into her suitcase and sent on with the casket; some clothing was distributed along Sixth Street, worn out and turned into dust rags, quilt scraps. Untraceable bits and pieces. It didn't take long to clean up after her. She had only passed through.

How could I reconstruct what had hardly existed?

There were two photos. Gram had placed them on my dresser on the day I came to stay for good, the day they found her body. One was a snapshot of my mother and father together. She leaned toward him; his arm was laid lazily along her shoulders. They both were resting against a shiny black car. The car was the focus of the photograph, Uncle Sam's brand new 1935 Cadillac. At the far left of the photo, the smiling couple was small and insignificant against the bulk and brilliance of the car. Around its solidity the world was liquid. My mother's print dress tugged at her; my father's shirtsleeve was caught in mid flap. That Taylor wind blew. Cottonwoods streamed at the upper edge of the photo, at the bottom the earth itself was on the move. You could almost taste the bitter grit in their tiny white smiles, feel the dust sting as they squinted valiantly into the camera. The other shot was a wedding photo of her. She was caught in angled light. Her head bent, most of her face was in shadow. Light planed across high cheekbones and forehead, searched the sweeping tips of her dark lashes and lingered in the smooth hair pulled back by a glittering clip. She was gazing down at the shimmering length of her dress. In the background, blurred and in darkness, was my father. I recognized the set of his shoulders, the jut of his chin. He stood ready to stride into the game and win for the home team. It was not a candid shot. It was posed, artistic, the husband, the bride, the exchange of light and dark. What did she see, looking down at herself like that, I wondered, a shimmering length of skirt? Or did she look beyond the hem, to some other edge that only she could see?

Josie was no help.

Too young, she said dismissively when I asked her what

she remembered.

For Josie, childhood had been several lifetimes ago. My uncles Stan, Sam, and Mike were worse. They shook their heads, shrugged, and looked away. They didn't want to tell me what they really remembered, what they thought I didn't know. There had been bets taken at the Taylor Club: Jumped or Fell. Odds ran about even until everyone lost interest. That left my aunts—Anna, Mimi, and Kiki. They usually had something to say about everything, but on the subject of my mother, they had always been silent. I'm sure they thought that dying like that was unaccountable, even treasonous. The family closed over that wound. There wasn't even a scar. We all moved on.

I longed for Gram. She would have told me. She understood about appeasing ghosts. The desire to know, to understand had come too late. She was gone.

I sat at the kitchen table at Aunt Anna's, helping her form meatballs for a birthday dinner for Sofie. The sticky meat mixture coated my hands as I rolled globs between my palms, then placed the finished balls on a plate to be dropped into hot oil by Aunt Anna until they were crusty and brown, ready to be added to the bubbling sauce. I had already written down the recipe for future use. Josie loved spaghetti and meatballs, and had even deigned to come to her mom's house for dinner that evening, seeing that it was a special occasion. Uncle Nick had come home for lunch and had brought Milan with him. They sat in companionable quiet, Uncle Nick reading the sports page and Milan chewing his sandwich with methodical precision. At the stove, Aunt Anna grumbled at her meatballs, which were sticking, and adjusted the heat.

What was she like? I asked.

The two men raised their heads and gazed at me with placid, bovine faces. Milan still chewed. Aunt Anna turned from the stove, waving her spatula in irritated inquiry.

She, who?

My mom.

Aunt Anna stared. Behind her the meatballs spat and crackled and settled into stubborn adherence with the bottom of the iron skillet.

Fine. A chuvar. Why?

Just wondering, I said, concentrating on the sphere of pink meat in my hands.

So, what was she like, then?

I said. A chuvar. When she came here to teach, she couldn't pronounce anybody's name.

Aunt Anna muscled the meatballs around the pan and recited a litany of names from around the neighborhood:

Colliopolous, Draconovich, Piscovitic, Antrocelli... .

Was she beautiful?

I thought of black curls and dimples, violet eyes... Not my mother, but someone's.

Aunt Anna shrugged.

So, why did my dad marry her?

Aunt Anna didn't answer. Instead, she jabbed the sizzling, browned meatballs with a long-handled meat fork and dropped them one by one into the thick red sauce. Uncle Nick leaned forward over his forgotten paper and said in a low voice,

They danced...

Aunt Anna turned quickly to glare at him, waving her fork menacingly. Uncle Nick swallowed convulsively, watching Anna warily, but continued,

...while they were going together. Every Friday, Saturday night, in Parker. The Nevada Club. Sometimes I'd see... .

I'll tell you why he married her, Aunt Anna burst angrily. *He married her because nobody could tell your dad a damn thing! That's why! He should have married somebody from Sixth Street like I told him.*

Anna... Uncle Nick soothed.

Oh shut up, You.

Furiously Aunt Anna turned her back on us. She stirred the spaghetti sauce with murderous intent. Meatballs rode the crest of her anger, careening around the pot and sinking helplessly. We three sat at the table, waiting in silence for her to subside. Uncle Nick rediscovered his newspaper. Milan took a paper napkin from the holder on the table and, producing a grease pencil from his shirt pocket, began to draw.

Am I like her? I asked, clearly enough to be heard over the pot banging.

It was a long time ago, Anna answered with finality. The frying pan smoked.

Get a move on. I'm all out of meatballs here.

Watching Aunt Anna's back, Milan slid the napkin over the table to me.

I make shoes, he murmured.

His voice was so quiet, I thought for a moment he hadn't spoken at all. But on the white napkin next to my elbow was a drawing of a shoe. It sported an elegant, narrow heel of a medium height and an open toe. A dancing shoe.

Best cowhide. Size four. Blue.

I imagined them the color of a robin's egg, holding rapturous movement in their delicate confines, sailing over a worn, wooden floor, dancing to the edge of the world.

Mimi and Kiki fidgeted nervously on their couch.

So long ago, Mimi complained.

Yes, too long, Mimi, Kiki agreed, patting Mimi's knee reassuringly.

Mama wouldn't like it. She wouldn't want us bringing up all that old stuff. Would she, Kiki?

Kiki nodded, still patting Mimi's knee.

Gram wouldn't mind. She'd understand, I urged.

Mama always said, 'Keep agoin.' That means not stirring the past, doesn't it Kiki.

No, I think she meant... I began and then gave up.

They were smiling and nodding their heads vigorously at each other. Their eyes sparkled with tears.

Keep agoin... Yes, yes. That certainly was Mama, wasn't it, Kiki?

Oh yes,Mimi. She always said that. Keep agoing. I remember... .

I just want to know about her, Aunt Kiki, I cut in firmly. *She was my mom, Aunt Mimi.*

No, no! Mimi said firmly. *Gram was your mama. Wasn't she, Kiki?*

Yes, she might as well have been, Mimi! Gram was your mama, Mala.

Becky, Kiki, Mimi corrected gently. *Josie wants us to call her Becky.*

Oh yes, Mimi. I forgot. Thank you. Becky. Gram took care of you, Becky.

Except for in the beginning.

Yes, just the very beginning.

Six weeks. That's not so much. Don't you agree, Kiki?

No, not much at all, Mimi.

We all stirred our coffee in quiet speculation.

Then that terrible accident, Kiki whispered.

Maybe no accident, Kiki, Mimi countered. *Maybe she jumped.*

Oh no, Mimi, Kiki gasped and put her hand over her mouth. *I know they said that,Mimi. But surely not. No one we know would do that!*

That's just it, Kiki. We never knew her.

Well, but, Mimi. She...

What was she doing always climbing that cliff? Nobody climbs cliffs, Mimi insisted belligerently.

I'm sure people climb cliffs someplace, Mimi.

Not here, Kiki!

The bootlegger climbed that cliff, Mimi. What about the

bootlegger?

That was his work!

Maybe she...

She was just trying to get above us, always sneaking up there! Mimi insisted angrily. *That's what I say. And it serves her right!*

Mimi! Shame!

Shocked by disagreement, they inched away from each other on the couch. Disloyalty loomed in front of them, dark and unknown. Their twin hairdos trembled, and they blinked at each other in confusion.

I just want to know what she was like, I said quietly into the space between them.

It was all a long time ago!

With those words, Mimi stomped into the kitchen, her cup and saucer rattling like broken bones in a bag. Kiki jumped up and rushed after her. I sat in the sudden quiet of the front room, looking down into my empty cup. The sound of urgent whispering came from the kitchen. Aunt Kiki emerged

Mala, er...Becky I mean, Mimi...I...we need to go to the shops for some things... Aunt Kiki's voice trailed off uncomfortably.

Aunt Kiki, I'm sorry...

Aunt Kiki bobbed her head and with quick, precise movements eased me towards the door. She peeked back at the kitchen, where the sound of washing dishes could be heard. Surreptitiously, she ducked outside with me.

Once, she whispered, putting her hand up to her mouth for added precaution.

Once, she corrected Mimi's English.

She blinked at me with bright, sad eyes and nodded her hairdo gravely.

It was all such a long time ago.

I walked home through hot, stinging dust, through a town shuttered and closed against invasion. I wished my friend

Carrie more luck than I had had and contemplated the slight knowledge I'd gained. I weighed the cost. What was left: two photos, black and white; a white napkin, on it a delicately drawn shoe, size four, blue; an insistence on correct English, an inability to pronounce foreign names; a weakness for heights and maybe an untamed man; a love of dancing...falling... .

11

It took a nuclear test and the new sheriff's arrival to shift the town's attention away from Doctor Price.

For the first event there were few witnesses: the milkman, rattling around in his truck, leaving glass bottles in sets of four on dark front porches; the paperboy, still groggy with sleep, rolling newspapers in the dew-wet yard; and the men on the early shift, walking quietly past silhouetted trees and houses, through air the color and texture of a dove's wing, along the scattered streets of town to a new day's work. Only birds registered a response. When the southeastern sky exploded from behind the black shelf of cliffs with a sudden searing white light that for lingering moments vaporized the pre-dawn dimness, the birds rose en masse, screaming. They streamed through the sky, black fluid spilt on bright, false day. The humans had seen it all before. There was no mushroom cloud, no painful column of eviscerated earth erupting in the air. We were too far away for that. Early watchers experienced only this rare brilliance, the signature of man in the heavens. They watched the light and the birds subside and then calmly went on with their day, first closing their eyes for a moment to adjust to the settling darkness.

At 10:00 a.m. the wind changed. The flag above the post office fluttered and dipped, dancing its way around the pole until it streamed and snapped at the northwest. It meant the day would be cooler, the wind traveling over high rocky peaks and pine-covered ridges to reach Taylor. No afternoon dust storm to send us inside, it was a perfect day for a trip to the swimming pool, a perfect evening for baseball at the park. This pleasant breeze, on its path to our town, passed right over Yucca Flats, the Nevada Proving Grounds, two hundred miles away, where the military had just tested their nuclear bomb, releasing it into the atmosphere at 5:00 a.m. It was an unhappy coincidence, the change in wind and the test. Our prevailing winds were almost always from the northwest. A recurrent coincidence that had happened before. If all went according to schedule, we could expect the fallout starting at about three.

A few years before, the Basque sheepherders had brought the first stories to Taylor. They shook their heads sadly over kitchen tables as their wives dished up their first home-cooked meals in months. The sheep were sick, their wool falling out in heavy handfuls. Sores erupted on their pink hides and refused to heal. The lambs were the worst, born dead or with horrid deformities. These, the sheepherders had to kill themselves. The sheepherders looked at their callused hands and tucked them into their armpits and rocked with the memory.

As they threaded their lonely way through high green valleys and sage-covered plains they stopped in at settlements and homesteads and talked with ranchers and farmers. They heard about cattle dying and the strange behavior of crops. Then they brought their worries home and laid them down on the kitchen table for their wives to sort and mend with food and jug wine. Later, at the Taylor Club, worn boots angling from barstool rungs, they hunched over their whiskeys and muttered what they knew to listeners.

Sheriff Billy listened. Long before the government had acknowledged the existence of nuclear fallout, Sheriff Billy had devised a civil defense plan to protect his town. It gave him a chance to use his beloved bullhorn. When conditions aligned, when prevailing winds stilled and swung around and a pre-dawn light show attested to the military 'proving' something on Yucca Flats, Sheriff Billy whipped his bullhorn out of his locker at the jail and lumbered into action. We could hear him long before he ever reached our personal stretch of territory, Sixth Street. Crawling through town in his pickup, one hand on the wheel, a quart bottle of beer next to him, head and beefy shoulders wedged out of the open window, he bellowed through the bullhorn:

Those damn cusses are at it again! Better bring in your washing and your kids. Yucca Flats is on the rise!

Sheriff Billy received such intense enjoyment from this activity that he started to study weather on a global basis. What about those winds high up in the atmosphere you couldn't see? Sure, it's easy to tell which way the wind's blowing when it's hitting you in the face and turning your sweat to salt. But those winds way up there, they could be carrying any damn thing. Sheriff Billy began announcing every nuclear test, despite the direction of the flag on the pole above the post office. He also proclaimed election days, civic events, significant birthdays, and town league ballgame scores. Thereby, the populace of Taylor was well informed, and to Billy's thinking, safe. Some people listened to him; others thought him a fool.

Gram was one of the ones who listened. Sheriff Billy's truck always brought her to the screen door. As he crept past, Gram would squint at the blameless sky and shake her head.

That no damn good thing, she'd say.

Then she'd strip the sheets off her bed and take them outside to cover her vegetable garden. She'd sleep without sheets that night. She gave it twenty-four hours. In the afternoon of the following day she'd bring in the sheets, soak them in the bathtub in a combination of Ivory Flakes and Clorox, rinse them, and hang the on the line. By dark, they would be dry, soft from the wind's play and full of the tart smell of sage. We'd eat vine-ripened tomatoes or cucumbers and onions drenched in vinegar and salt, and Gram would nod her head in approval with every bite.

The invisible poison sifted down on us despite all efforts. It settled in our lawns where the children laughed and rolled like puppies. It mixed with the dust on the roads that every car kicked up in passing. It filtered into our drinking water. We swallowed it in great thirsty gulps. It layered itself on the desolate face of The Sands where every afternoon it was gathered up and flung back at us. It seasoned our dinners. It settled to the bottom of our spring-fed swimming pool and bubbled up to tease the cold toes of children paddling there. There were not enough Clorox and Ivory Flakes to wash it away.

Now Sheriff Billy was dead. His bullhorn lay snout down, on the top shelf of his abandoned locker. News of the test traveled idly through town as the day slipped by.

Should we pull in the laundry? the housewives asked each other over the back fence and glanced up at the sky.

What about the kids?

They're having such a good time down at the pool...

What did Sheriff Billy know anyhow?

A lot about women and whiskey, that's for sure...

Why, the government wouldn't be doing it, if it were bad...
Would they?

No. They wouldn't...

Even those who decided to play it safe, who bribed their children with ice cream to keep them indoors, came out anyway at 4:00 p.m., for town league baseball. Taylor was playing Pierstown, a hamlet at the far side of the copper pit. Pierstown had that Greek kid, a real slugger. Rumor was he could pitch, too. The two teams were tied for first, and they hadn't met each other this season. It was going to be a great ball game. The post office window was closed, and every shop on Main had a sign hung on the door: *'Back after the game'*. Some men slinked off their shift at the smelter. Everyone was going.

At the park, the bleachers were packed. Josie and I pried ourselves into the center of an enclave of uncles and aunts and squirming cousins. Aunt Anna took the opportunity to fuss at Josie's dress, which she thought too low in front.

You look thin, she said to me, as if I'd been on a long, hard voyage since I'd sat at her table three days before.

The game started; everyone shushed her. She managed to slip in a parting shot:

When I get you back in August, Mala, I'm going to feed you right up.

Her name's Becky, Ma, Josie parried. *She can feed herself. She's a great cook.*

Aunt Anna scowled at us across six cousins and an uncle. A resounding crack drew her attention to the game. The local crowd watched silently as the Pierstown Greek kid's ball arced and sailed over center field, heading for a front yard clear across the highway. Aunt Anna stood up.

Shame on you Eddie Pintar! Aunt Anna hollered and shook her finger at the pitcher. *What kind of pitch was that? You straighten up and play right! That goes for all of you!*

The action on the field wavered. The players in the infield stopped to listen to Aunt Anna. In the outfield, they looked to one another across green distances and shrugged, shaking their heads. Even the Greek kid in his triumphant circuit around the bases hesitated mid-stride rounding third, squinted up into the crowd, and then walked sedately into home. Josie's laughter glided out over the crowd and down to meet the Greek kid at the plate. Aunt Anna thumped back into her spot on the bleachers. One-Nothing, Visitors.

Halfway through the game, I noticed the sky. Like gauze caught in the slanting rays of the late afternoon sun, it shimmered and rippled above the park. Tiny rainbows sparked and shifted and disappeared. I thought of Gram's tomatoes, her peas and cucumbers and lettuce laying in long open rows down the side of the house. I nudged Josie and pointed to the glistening sky. Millions of particles of dust, unseen except for the way they caught the light, danced high in the breeze. They had traveled two hundred miles from the place of their birth in hot, blasted desert, then over cool rocky peaks and pine-covered ridges and finally over the cliff in back of our town to give this performance, a lesson in refraction right above our heads. Yucca Flats was on the rise. By twos and threes heads began to tilt back. The game on the field continued, the players crouched, intent in their sweaty, dirt-streaked uniforms. It was tight. Five-Four, Pierstown leading. The crowd divided its attention, catching the pitch, the swing of the bat, the slide to first, then, peering up, found glittering omens in the skies.

The crowd's attention shifted again. A blue Buick, sitting low on its wheels and dragging a tin-colored trailer, pulled into town. It traveled the highway behind left field, then center, and slowly turned the corner behind right and pulled up along the fence. It idled there about five minutes while the man and the boy in the gray interior and the crowd outside on their bleachers in the spotlight of the sun tried to size each other up. There were too many of us and too little of them seen for either to form any clear impression. The car pulled out and continued up the hill toward the smelter offices.

Dan Piscovitch hit a homerun with two men on base in the seventh, but in the top of the eighth, the Greek kid from Pierstown tied it up with another screamer over center field. Then Tommy Teravetti hit into a double play and our side was out. It was the top of the ninth, and the Taylor fans were still moaning when the blue Buick pulled up again, this time without its trailer.

The man who stepped out was tall and concave. Even though he had driven hours to reach Taylor, you could still see the sharp creases in his short shirtsleeves and down the front of his pants. His hair was cropped short, somewhere between white and platinum, iridescent as the afternoon sky. His pink, speckled scalp showed through. He was going to have trouble with our high-altitude sun; you could tell that right away.

Ignoring the game, he stood at the open gate of the park and surveyed the bleachers. His eyes paused for a second, and then, with long strides, he reached the bleachers and sprung up the first three rows. He grabbed Naked Sal by the elbow and dragged him from the stands. Naked Sal struggled for footing, the rough wood of the bleachers banging and scraping his shins. The Methodist-Minister-Without-a-Flock called feeble objections and cringed away from the sudden open spot next to him. Once the two men had reached the ground, the stranger hauled Naked Sal to his feet and marched him out of the park. The dust from Sal's hair and shoulders settled in their wake.

The game ceased; players and crowd blinked in shock. The last we saw of Sal was his grimy bum, quivering in terror, being shoved unceremoniously into the back of the Buick.

It was the first official act of our new sheriff. He hadn't even stopped to pick up his badge yet.

We lost the game. Pierstown collected two more runs. We couldn't seem to hold them. In the bottom of the ninth, we struck out one, two, three. Josie and I walked home in the glittering, milky twilight. At home, I stood in the yard and stared at the vegetables now deep in the slanting shade of Gram's house. Too late to take cover now, I thought. We're on our own.

Later that night, along hushed, dark streets, Carrie came to see us.

12

I want to know about her.

She was a silhouette on the other side of the screen door, a thin wisp of blue-gray smoke. I looked up from my book and Josie from her *Life* magazine. We could see the pink tips of her fingers pressed against the mesh. Yes, I thought.

Come in, said Josie.

Josie stood up as Carrie stepped in from the dark. She pointed Carrie to the couch and then flopped down into Eli's chair, swung her legs up over the arm, and dropped her magazine over the edge. The instant Carrie sat down her body tilted and slid awkwardly into Gram's hollow in the center of the couch, my territory. We sat shoulders and hips pressed together, two motherless girls in the grips of ancient brocade, looking to Josie for help. Josie was examining her red-tipped toes.

Why?

I just want to know about her, Carrie said stubbornly. Her violet eyes were dark. *She's probably my mom. Wouldn't you want to know about your mom, Josie? Wouldn't you want to know if you're like her?*

Yes, I answered her.

Josie stood up, towering over us.

I know. I am nothing like my mother. I'm me.

Josie arched her back and reached long arms toward the ceiling, stretching like a cat thoroughly pleased with itself.

I'm getting a soda. Anyone want one?

Me, Carrie and I chimed.

Watching her prowl down the hall, I turned to Carrie and muttered, *I've never met anyone more like her mother in my life.*

Carrie's grin was sudden and breathtaking. At once, she was my comrade again, not the pale child in the graveyard, not the hollow, aching voice across the copper phone line. She was the girl who stood beside me on the playground, facing down taunts. *Don't stand near Mala. It's enough to kill ya! That's right! Everybody's dying to get away from her!* She was Carrie the warrior, the girl with the mean right cross and the willingness to use it on anyone of any size. I watched the dimple deepen in her cheek. I was suddenly light with this small gift I had given her.

Sometimes it's good to be a little like your mom, I told her.

Josie was back from the kitchen with three root beers. The ice in the glasses made soft music in time to her steps. She handed out drinks, looking curiously at our smiles, and returned to her claim on Eli's chair.

How are you going to find out about her?

We could call on the phone, I offered.

Call The Green Willow?

Sure! We've—

I stopped. Carrie jabbed my ribs with a sharp elbow. Josie's eyebrows raised delicately. Josie, who was not anything like her mother, had also probably never been a kid either. She was looking at us speculatively, a smile slowly pulling up the corners of her mouth.

I bet, she suggested silkily. *I bet you two already know the number of The Green Willow by heart. In fact, I bet you know the numbers for all four of those whorehouses!*

Josie's voice was suddenly younger, disingenuous.

Hi! Is this The Green Willow? I'd like to apply for a job. What qualifications do I need?

Carrie and I were squirming uncomfortably in the close hollow of the couch.

I bet you've called those numbers hundreds of times...

We grinned sheepishly and tried to blink innocently out from deeply tinged faces.

I bet they might even recognize your voices.

Carrie and I collapsed against each other, thoroughly deflated. Josie laughed merrily, savoring the joke.

Did you think you invented that game?

She grinned like the Cheshire Cat.

I'll call, she stated simply.

Now?

Josie glanced at the clock on the wall: ten fifteen.

Tomorrow. They're busy now.

She scooped up *Life* from the floor beside her and smiled into a photo article about war brides.

Carrie and I were waiting for Josie when she came home from work. Carrie had spent the long afternoon with me. We had shopped and done laundry. By two o'clock we were trapped behind windows pelted with dust and sand. Outside, the cottonwoods sighed and bent, shaking dust from their leaves. I showed Carrie how to make bread and put her to work peeling potatoes while I cut deep slits into a leg of lamb and inserted garlic cloves.

I don't use garlic when I cook, she commented, watching me curiously.

Carrie cooked dinner for her father every worknight, a task she had taken over when she was eight. Eggs scrambled with cut-up hot dogs was her specialty. She never bothered with plates, just two forks and the pan in the center of the table. By Thursday night Dr. Price was gently suggesting Mrs. Miniverri's In-home Diner. Carrie admitted a need to branch out.

I use garlic all the time, I told her.

Dad doesn't like to smell like garlic when he's seeing patients.

For a moment it was as if we stared at each other across the gray expanse of Main Street. We were from two worlds separated by the center yellow line...and garlic.

Gram always said garlic cures everything...even a broken heart...

Carrie smiled and shrugged. *I better pick some up the next time I go shopping.*

We peeled carrots and cut onions into large chunks and put

everything in Gram's dented black roasting pan.

Lots of salt and pepper. That's the key, I told her.

I'm going to write all this down, Carrie decided and wandered into my room to find a pad and pencil.

By the time Josie walked in the front door, the house was redolent with baked bread and roasting lamb, the kitchen faintly blue with the smoke from sizzling fat.

God, that smells good, she said, announcing her arrival.

First you have to call, Josie, said Carrie. *You promised.*

The roast needs another half-hour anyway, I added.

Josie sat at the kitchen table and waved absent-mindedly at the smoke. She pulled the phone across the table and stared at it while Carrie and I hovered over her anxiously. She picked up the heavy black receiver and then set it back into the cradle. She drummed her fingers lightly on the wood of the table.

Got it, she smiled to herself. *Number?*

329-4726, Carrie and I yelled together in a rush of freed breath.

Josie flipped back her hair with a toss of her head and picked up the receiver again. She dialed the number slowly, dragging her nail along the circular path of the dial, pausing an instant after each recoil.

Come on! Carrie whispered urgently.

Slouched in her chair, Josie wouldn't be hurried. She was still considering. At last, the dial settled back in place for the last time. We could hear faint ringing, each ring slow and the gap between endless, then the low hum of a male voice.

Hello. Am I speaking to the manager of The Green Willow?

Everyone knew the setup at the local whorehouses. The owner was usually the manager, accountant, bartender, cook, and dishwasher. Low overhead. The only other male voice you might encounter on the line was the bouncer's. But that was seldom. Bouncers were silent towers of muscle. The only indication they were alive were the movement of their eyes as they watched customers from the stool by the door and the occasional burst of energy when they heaved the ill-behaved out-side and stalked out after the airborne body.

Yes. My name is Samantha MacNair...

I gaped at Josie. Carrie grinned. Josie's voice was smooth and low, utterly professional. Her posture changed. She sat for-ward, squaring her shoulders, straightening her spine. I could see the woman she would be after her years in college and Taylor far behind her.

I'm a journalist for Life Magazine. Perhaps you've seen my work? The latest issue...war brides?

Josie ran a fingernail idly along a scratch in the table.

Pick it up. You'll enjoy it.

I was grinning now too. Josie winked.

Anyway, Mr. Oaks...may I call you Neal? ...I'm doing some preliminary research for an article on legalized prostitution in Nevada. I've already spoken to the people over at the Wild Filly Ranch near Reno. You've heard of it?

She pronounced Nevada with a long a, like an Easterner, a nice touch. Carrie ran from the room with her hand over her mouth.

I wanted the perspective of smaller establishments, too. I'm hoping you can help me Neal, Josie purred.

There is another low hum from the phone. Josie smiled and reached for the pad and pencil. She tucked Carrie's recipe for bread and roast leg of lamb under the back of the pad. She wrote *Green Willow* across the top and quickly sketched slen-der branches and narrow leaves sprouting from the words.

It's a fascinating subject, Neal. Don't you think?

Josie listened to the voice on the other end of the line. Standing just behind her, I could almost hear the swagger in the low bursts of sound that traveled the line and into our kitchen.

Just a few questions, Neal. How many, uh, ladies does The Green Willow employ? ...Really? What are their ages? Oh, I see. Believe me, Neal, I understand thoroughly, Josie chuckled softly. *That's women for you, Neal.*

From the other end of the line came a light, low burping sound. Neal was laughing appreciatively.

What are their wages, Neal?

Josie' eyebrows rose.

How many customers do they usually have a night?

Josie pursed her lips but suppressed the whistle. She tapped the tip of the pencil on the pad, wrote a number down, and circled it darkly. She doodled large dollar signs around the page, gave them quick flourishes in heavy lead.

That's quite impressive, Neal. I'm wondering...do you have an order in which the ladies receive customers? I mean, do they take turns, or do they have regulars? How does that work, Neal?

There was a long explanation on the other end of the line. Carrie crept back into the kitchen. Josie looked up, noticing Carrie, remembering suddenly why she was calling.

Is there a favorite among the ladies? Someone who's always in demand?

Josie already knew the answer. Carrie slid noiselessly into the chair next to her. On the pad, Josie wrote in bold dark capitals, THE DIVINE. The air in the kitchen was thick and hot, tasting of grease and salt.

Surely that's not her real name. Can I have that information?

Josie listened and shook her head at Carrie.

Yes, that's understandable, she said to Neal. *Well, answer me this: How does someone like The Divine become so famous?*

There was a long explanation. While she listened and nodded, Josie sketched a face, a close likeness to Carrie. Lovely. In the process of darkening the loose curls around the face, Josie paused, pencil poised. A slight blush crept up the arched column of her neck. She blinked, the curls forgotten. I looked at Carrie. In the smoky, darkening kitchen, her face was pale, the planes of her cheeks open, empty, waiting for a mark. I decided it was time to take the roast out of the oven and busied myself with finding hot pads. I opened the oven door. A rich, moist haze engulfed me, obscuring everything around me.

We need to get some fresh air in here, I choked, waving at the air and rushing to the windows. Josie cleared her throat delicately.

How long has she been with you? Josie asked.

On the line, there was a considering pause, a short answer. Josie, pencil still poised, wrote nothing down. Her brown eyes narrowed slowly. Smoke drifted toward the open window and the tart scent of wet sagebrush mingled with the pungency of garlic, lamb and fresh, hot bread. Somewhere rain nourished a land.

How would she feel about an interview?

The answer was monosyllabic.

I see. Well, thank you, Neal. You've been very helpful.

Josie hung up and sat back in her chair, staring down at the pad thoughtfully.

Can you go see her? Carrie whispered into the silence.

No.

What do you mean? You didn't find out anything, Josie, Carrie protested and pointed to the pad.

Josie watched the disappointment and frustration play across Carrie's face. She looked down at the pad: a number, some dollar signs, a lovely face half finished, a name holding in its six letters all the inaccessibility of Heaven, and *Green Willow* with its filigree of vines and leaves. She pulled the top sheet out from underneath the pad and covered her work with Carrie's recipes for hand-made bread, lamb with lots of garlic. She smiled gently at Carrie.

We know she's probably one of the richest women in the county. And there's something else. How long have you and your dad been here?

Six years this summer.

Well, she's been here not quite six and a half. She came in February of the same year. I think your dad must have found her and followed her here.

In the quiet kitchen, Josie reached over and took Carrie's hand. The pan of roast and brown vegetables was unaccountably heavy in my hands. I could feel the heat of it through the ancient hot pads. My voice was barely more than a whisper.

We need to eat.

Stay and eat, Carrie, Josie urged. *We'll go to the drug store for a float after.*

Carrie nodded, the movement of her head a slight tremble. She was pale and empty, so we would fill her up with lamb and potatoes, with carrots and crisped curls of onions, with bread that was like an offering to heaven, with lots and lots of garlic. As we sat and chewed silently, there were four of us at the table: two girls, a young woman, and the specter of a man. He spent his time patiently caring for the sick of this little town and in the company of his only daughter. He ate scrambled eggs with chunks of hot dogs without a plate. He remembered, followed, waited. Thirty miles away the woman lay like an exotic dish, casting her rich spicy scent onto the cooling breeze.

Later, we walked home from the soda fountain past the Taylor Club where the thick hunched shapes of old men lined the sidewalk benches on either side of the bright, welcoming rectangle. The sound of laughter and drinking escaped from inside, a sound like shattering glass in the hushed town. Carrie, reluctant to return home, accompanied us. Bats cloaked in a deeper shade of night dipped and swerved through the dark. They dived toward our heads, making us duck. The beat of their wings stirred the air around our ears and cheeks. At the front gate, Carrie hesitated. Josie slipped inside the house. I stood beside Carrie, waiting.

I've decided, she said in a low voice.

She reached out and grasped me above the elbows.

I'm going to go see her. Meet me at the railroad tracks tomorrow at one.

Silhouetted in the darkness before me, her hair the breeze-tossed black of nocturnal wings, she didn't wait for an answer. She knew I would come. We were comrades. She turned and walked away into a night turbulent with flight.

13

The trick was to jump onto the train just as it left the smelter gate, to hide in the waist-deep sagebrush along the tracks, to catch the ore cars as they slid out onto the open plain on their return trip to the pit. There was very little room between the jutting edge of the cars and the tangled, gray-green verge. There was very little time. It took an eruption of pounding feet and a sudden leap of panicked commitment to launch a body toward the rungs that climbed the middle of the ore cars. As the train picked up speed, sweaty fingers strengthened by desperation clung to the sun-hot rung while legs combed back by the rushing wind peddled over blurred branches, climbing air, struggling for a toehold. Then up the side, rung by rung, shaking at a pitch that matched the agitated car, and over the side, to elation in the dusty, empty calm. Every few years, a young adventurer on an impromptu trip to Parker would trip over sagebrush, misjudge a dive, or slip helplessly from the rungs of an ore car and roll under the wheels of the train. The trip ended at the cemetery, closed casket funeral, a set of parents broken, too. Train jumping was the one activity that landed a kid in Sheriff Billy's jail with the cell door closed, the weight of Billy's disapproval crowding the tight space and using all the available oxygen.

We could only guess what the new sheriff might do.

In my family, train jumping was a Family Crime. Any act that carried the potential of needless grief or shame to the family was a Family Crime. To have been caught committing a Family Crime meant a dip into the icy waters of total, silent isolation. Encased in disgrace, you were nobody, nothing, for days, weeks, months. Even the sympathetic wouldn't talk to you, in case the horrible banishment was catching. Climbing mountains that could then be jumped or fallen from was obviously a Family Crime. Rushing a beach, as my dad had, in the face of inevitable, killing enemy fire was not. That was duty, heroism. Jumping a train with Carrie to visit a whore was in the no-man's land between extremes, between friendship and foolishness. It was best to not be caught.

Carrie took the second car, I the third. Once inside, she scrambled up the sloping back of her car, negotiated the rocking, narrow space between our two cars, and slid down next to me. We dragged air into our scalding lungs, listened to our hearts pound, and tried to sense through our vibrating bones the sickening drop of speed that meant we had been seen and were in deep, deep trouble.

We're safe, I hollered finally over the rumble of the cars and the metallic grind of the wheels.

Carrie nodded. Around us, copper dirt hung in the air and danced like green dervishes on the car's surfaces. It collected in riveted junctions, in dents and hollows, prancing out again with every new jog of the tracks.

We're going to be filthy by the time we get there, Carrie complained loudly and brushed at the green dirt that clung to her dress and bare legs. Brushing at it only ground it in.

You might as well wait 'til we get there to do that, I pointed out.

Carrie gave up, wrapped arms around shins and pressed her closed eyes into her kneecaps. I cranked my head up and watched the clean sky through the green curtain as long as I could stand it, then followed Carrie's example and closed my eyes against the roiling dust. Green grains still gathered and danced ecstatically behind my eyelids. Twenty-five miles per hour. It would take us a little over an hour to reach Parker, over an hour spent in hot, rumbling darkness in the belly of the train, tensing slowly for the whistle that announced the approach of town, for the drop in speed, the scramble up and over the side, the heart-stopping jump and roll through scratching brush, for the too short walk through town to the dead-end street with its knot of dingy, knowing brothels. Over an hour to worry about what came next.

What are we going to do when we get there? I asked into the void beyond my eyelids.

I could feel the lift of Carrie's shoulder next to mine, a silent, terse shrugging off of possibilities.

We need a plan, Carrie. What if...

I'm seeing her, Carried stated.

What are you going to say?

I'm going to say... to ask... I... I want to know...

There was too much to ask. Sitting next to her in our enforced darkness, I felt the almost physical struggle as she sought words.

I just want to see her, she said finally.

I peeked at her. Her back, curved and taunt as a bowstring, vibrated at a higher frequency than the loose-jointed train that carried us. She seemed held together by a tiny, tough knot of need. I wanted to reach out and clutch her, to ease her somehow. I closed my eyes again. A little less than an hour now, I thought to myself.

What will she be like...The Divine? I tested the words on my dry tongue.

Carrie was silent. So much depended on it.

Gram told me a story once about a whore...uh, prostitute. She was good.

There was no response, no indication she had heard me or accepted my offering. But I would tell the story anyway, fill distance and time with words that were harmless. I raised my voice above the wind and let the rhythm of the train work its way up through the soles of my sandals, into my bones and belly and lungs. My words spun with the rhythm in my throat, dervishes, green and hopeful.

There was a mining town way up high in the mountains in Colorado where Gram lived with my real grandfather, before he died and she came here.... It was in the middle of nowhere and so close to the tree line that every rock and boulder was cracked by frost. When Gram first moved there, she didn't know that frost could do that. She thought giants walked there. She watched for them.

I glanced over at Carrie. Her eyes pressed closed on the bones of her knees, she was still.

It's not anything that happened when Gram lived there. It's a story from way before, a hundred years ago, when the town was filled with prospectors. They came from all over the world, digging holes in the mountainside, searching for gold.

Anyway, there was this prostitute who lived in the town. She was the only woman in the whole town. She was beautiful, Gram said. She was the most important person in that town. Every miner's best friend, every man's lover. The men fought over her with pistols; they gambled every bit of their stake for some time with her. They went without food, they even died for her. Her name was Rose, or something like that...some kind of flower. When Gram told me the story, I remember thinking that it was a flower that wouldn't ever grow at that altitude... .

I took another peek at Carrie. She had turned her head; her eyes were open, watching me. Green dust outlined each eyelash.

Well, one day a sick miner dragged into town from somewhere else. He had smallpox I think, something horrible like that. His face was covered with running sores and he was delirious with fever. They laid him out on the bar. Everyone wanted to get a look at him. It was like a circus had come to town. He didn't last for more than a day or two, but that didn't matter because before long everyone was sick, one hundred and fifty men laying in lonely, nasty little shacks scattered all over the mountainside. The closest doctor was fifty miles away. All they had was Rose.

I held Carrie's gaze for a moment.

She did it, Carrie. She took care of all of them. She fed them on soup she made and whiskey. She nursed back to health the ones she could. She dug graves for the ones that died. She

finally got sick herself while the ones that were left were recu-
perating. She locked herself into her house and closed the
blinds. When the few men who were well enough to get out of
bed came to check on her, she wouldn't let them in. She didn't
want them to see her. One night she just slipped away.

Did they ever find her?

I shook my head.

The miners searched for her. They sent word out to the
other mining camps in the area, but they never heard of her
again. She had disappeared.

What happened to her?

Gram always thought she probably climbed up into some
pass and died.

Why did she do that? The miners would have taken care of
her, Carrie protested.

Maybe. Maybe that's not what she wanted.

That's so sad, Carrie murmured and pressed her eyes back
into her knees.

I don't know. Think of what she did, saving all those min-
ers. Gram said there was a historical marker in the center of
town. *Big and bronze.* Gram couldn't read it, but everyone told
and retold the story. Gram always ended by saying, *'That*
damn good woman, strong.'

We spent the last few miles quietly. I sat hearing Gram's
voice, aching for the way she told that story, better than I had,
shaping and firming the words with her hands, offering truths
like slices of warm bread, simple and satisfying. Perhaps, sitting next to me, Carrie was imagining her mother, cast as Rose,
a beautiful flower that bloomed for a short time in a landscape
of shattered rock.

The train finally slowed, lurched us from our private
thoughts. We scrambled up the inside wall of the car and down
the ladder, leaping one at a time into the dirt on the verge.
Momentum rolled us off into the sagebrush and tumbleweed.
Hugging each other, then running towards the first straggling

buildings of Parker, we laughed and whooped in nervous triumph at a successful, safe escape. Hiding behind Harold's Feed and Paint, we surveyed the damage. I had a scraped knee and a torn sleeve; Carrie's hem had pulled loose in the tumble, and she was limping slightly. We were utterly filthy. Green.

Oh my God! Carrie moaned, looking first at me and then down at herself.

We worked on each other, brushing and rubbing, brushing again. A cloud of sickly dust settled in thin layers around our feet.

I think we might be dirtier than Naked Sal, Carrie commented.

That's not possible, I pointed out. *Besides, we're a different color.*

After all that rubbing and brushing, the best we could accomplish was a buffed, sickly green finish. Copper dirt. We looked like a couple of odd statues that had been thrown out to the mercy of the elements.

It's not even a pretty color, Carrie lamented, holding out her arms to examine them.

Maybe we should... We could come back, maybe hitch-hike....

No! We got this far alive. We're seeing her, Mala.

Becky, I corrected as she grabbed my wrist and dragged me around the building. She flashed me a jittery grin, white teeth rimmed in green.

Sure. Change colors and the next thing you know people think they have to have a new name! Come on then, Becky!

I laughed with the biting edge of nerves and ran a few steps so we could walk side by side. I held her hand.

We chose to walk Second Street instead of Main. Its minor shops and little bars were mostly deserted in the hot afternoon sun. The few who saw us through grimy windows watched us curiously, two green girls on a mission. We started out determined and brisk, but as we neared our destination each step took more effort that the last. When we turned the corner to the unnamed street where the whorehouses clustered, we stalled, robbed of conviction. Along the perimeter of the short street, the whorehouses stood docile in the afternoon sun: The YumYum Tree, The Big Smile, The Green Willow, and Number 45.

No cars parked along the sides of the four buildings; no sign of life emitted through open windows or front doors. This time of day trade was at a standstill. Time seemed suspended on the rising heat waves from the street. Another few hours would see an influx of cars, loud music, blaring lights, laughter, liquor, sex.

Now what? I asked nervously.

Carrie licked her lips and whispered, *The Green Willow's the nicest, don't you think?*

The Green Willow was the only one with a lick of paint. It was a blazing white in a street of worn, gray clapboard. Bright green shutters trimmed each window. An entrancing hand had used the same glossy green to paint branches with narrow leaves arching over the door to meet at the boldly lettered name above.

Yes. How are we going to get in? I urged.

They probably get the best customers, too.

The best, Carrie. How are we going to get in?

Carrie still hesitated, considering the open windows, the gaping door. She filled her lungs with dusty, hot air, let it out with a shaky whistle.

We're going to walk in the front door. I guess.

Together, we stepped into the deep gutter and angled across the street straight for the deceptive oasis of painted branches and dark door beneath. The bouncer was not on duty yet; his stool braced the open glass door. Inside the bar, slanting sun trapped dust on every surface, highlighted black scuff marks on the floor. The bartender sat at a table, feet up, reading the paper, a cup of cold coffee at his side. His back was to the door.

We stood and watched him read the sports page, waiting to be noticed.

*Excuse me...*Carrie finally forced the words out through a tight throat.

The man looked over his shoulder. Balding, pink-faced with red-rimmed eyes, this must be Neal. I thought of his burping, flattered laugh, his oily voice across thirty miles of phone line. I tasted sharp copper in my mouth.

What you doing in here? You two can't be in here!

I...we came to see my mother, Carrie stuttered.

Neal set down his paper carefully; his feet plopped one at a time to the floor; he swiveled slowly to catch a good look at us.

Your mother? She from Mars or something? Neal snickered.

Carrie crossed her green arms across her thin chest.

The Divine, she said into the quiet hollow of the barroom.

Neal stood and walked slowly across to us. Each step rapped the floor. He wasn't much taller than we were, but he had all the height of age, ownership, and meanness.

The Divine, repeated Carrie.

Neal bent over a little and stared right into Carrie's face, their noses almost touching. Carrie wouldn't blink to satisfy him.

Let them come up, Neal.

A voice floated down the stairs. Called from her room by her name on unfamiliar lips, the woman stood at the gallery banister, her lovely face floating above a voluminous white negligee. I felt a tremor in Carrie's hand as she looked up. Her jaw dropped, and her breath escaped her in a long *ahhh.*

But Divine, they can't...

Now.

She was gone. The word drifted out an open doorway along the gallery. Neal straightened and swept his left arm out in coarse invitation toward the stairs. As Carrie pulled me forward, I watched Neal's hard little eyes and pinched face, pink as a new penny, until I tripped on the bottom step. I struggled for balance as Carrie dragged me up the stairs, drawn up on an invisible line.

The Divine had a corner room with three windows, two west, one south. Against the remaining wall was an unmade double bed and nightstand cluttered with scrunched tissues, a beer bottle, a hand-held mirror. The room was big enough for her to have a sofa and lounge chair with a small, low coffee table between. The table bristled with empty bar glasses and a heavy, black ashtray brimming with butts. Over the stale odor of old cigarettes and glasses glazed with dried whiskey or gin, the room smelled strangely of spring, of rich, wet, newly warmed earth, of too-sweet narcissus and hyacinth. The Divine's scent. Promise hung in the air like a fog.

She had arranged herself on the couch. Her face was perfect, each lash tipped in black, brows plucked and arched, lids shaded a deep gray, cheeks rouged and powdered, lips drawn scarlet. The sight of her in her cloud of white chiffon with pearly toes peeking from the hem felled Carrie. The Divine indicated the lounge chair with a slight movement of glossy curls. Carrie collapsed into it, sinking into its down cushion until the soles of her dirty shoes rose from the floor. The woman reached a translucent arm out and picked up a gently smoking cigarette from the overburdened tray. Her long nails held the same opalescent sheen as her toes. A long ash fluttered from the glowing tip as she pulled deeply on the cigarette. She waved lazily, once. As bidden, the ash floated harmlessly past her, settling on the carpet beside the couch.

You're green, she observed coolly, shooting a stream of smoke through brilliant lips.

Carrie was motionless, silent, robbed of words and will.

We rode the ore cars to get here, I told her, the taste of copper in my voice.

She shifted her focus to me.

Who are you?

Mala...Becky.

She looked away, toward the window where sheer curtains murmured fitfully. She drew on her cigarette, held it, released it, sucked it back in through open red lips, and let it curl from her nostrils. Carrie breathed in and out with her, her questions escaping without voice in a sigh of smoke. The woman's violet eyes traveled to Carrie's. They watched each other. All that was not asked, all that was not offered, drifted on the thick air.

The room set my teeth on edge—the mingling smells of sweet and sour, the tumbled bed, the used tissues and glasses, the heaping ashtray, the woman whose lacquered mask mimicked and mocked my friend. I stood behind Carrie's chair, clutching it, silently urging her to say anything, fighting on her behalf the press of the littered room, the cool retreat of this woman; losing on all fronts.

I'm expecting someone, The Divine said, checking a thin gold watch on a pale wrist, then reaching down to stub out the short, unfiltered cigarette butt. *A customer.*

I wondered who would clean up this room. Someone else. She locked eyes with me.

Take Karina home. Don't come back.

She looked away. In the absence of her gaze, I pulled Carrie to her feet and guided her from the room. I helped her negotiate the short gallery and the stairs. Behind us, the door to The Divine's room clicked closed. Carrie felt insubstantial in my guiding hands, made of thin smoke. From behind the bar, Neal watched our progress and polished the bar's oak finish to a dull sheen reflecting his distorted, coppery face aged by grained wood.

What did you expect, huh? Now get the hell out, he said nastily. *Before some cop catches you in here.*

I left Carrie beside the open door and walked back to the bar.

I'm going to use your phone.

He silently weighed his resistance against my stubbornness, then slid the phone across the bar. I dialed, listened to four rings...

Taylor Dry Goods.

Josie, we're in Parker, I said simply.

Silence.

I'll borrow a car. Go to the drugstore on Main and order something. I'll pay for it when I get there. Forty-five minutes.

She hung up.

Thanks, I said into the buzzing receiver and placed it into its cradle. I walked to the door and gathered up Carrie.

Now get the hell out, echoed Neal, but his voice had lost its venom. *What the hell did they expect?* he grumbled to himself.

I walked Carrie to the drugstore on the corner of Main and sat her on a yellow and chrome stool. I ordered two floats and put Carrie's straw in for her and gently slid the swirling mix of sharp, dark root beer and pure white ice cream toward her. In silence, we pulled the sweet, thick jumble through red and blue striped straws. We let each mouthful sit next to our tongues and mix with saliva until it lost its appeal, then we swallowed and pulled in more. Josie came, slapped two quarters down on the counter, and shepherded us to the running car. She executed a U-turn on the spot and headed back toward Taylor, watching us in the rearview mirror sitting in the deep back seat of Uncle Sam's old, black Cadillac. Carrie looked out her side window, watching the empty miles pass. I traced woven green lines on the palms of my hands, left for what you're born with, right for your future. Head line, heart line, life line, a linkage of possibilities....

Ore cars? Josie asked into the silence of the back seat ten miles out of Parker.

I nodded.

Family Crime. Clean up as soon as we get home. In the rearview mirror I saw her smiling to herself.

Five miles later, as we passed the Yellow Bird Halfway Diner, she began again, impatiently:

Well? What happened?

Nothing happened, I said quietly, trying to keep the frustration out of my voice.

What was she like, then?

I sighed, smelled smoke in the back of the car.

Let's just say she wasn't the type to save a townful of dying miners.

Josie frowned into the rectangle of the mirror.

What?

She saved all these miners, Gram said.

What are you talking about? Who?

Rose, I said miserably.

Carrie turned her head and looked at me. An invisible hand brushed gently over her face, leaving a small, dazed smile that tugged at the edges of her mouth and made the mustache of dried root beer fuzz quiver on her upper lip. A small dent appeared on the fresh green surface of her left cheek. It flexed, trembled, deepened a little.

She knew my name.

I blinked at her, uncomprehending.

She called me Karina.

Names are small things, a word or two, nothing more. But there is potency to them, the hope of fiction, the solidity of truth. Whore, mother, friend. Moia Mala, 'my little one'. Becky, Carrie Price, Rose, Karina... Divine. Each name filled with the magic and rich texture of an entire history. I understood about names. More than the worn plaid upholstery of the Cadillac's back seat or its liquid, rocking ride, the significance of names cushioned the rest of our ride home.

14

I walked in the front door with a bag of groceries. Josie was already home, inhabiting Eli's chair with her Coke and magazine. She saluted me with a tip of the sweating bottle.

Here you are.

Uncle Nick sat in the deep spot on Gram's couch, his clean, barber's hands folded and quiet in his lap. He nodded his head, solemnly agreeing with Josie's observation. Not a hair moved. Except when drunk, Uncle Nick was a walking advertisement for his craft. His hair, graying now around the temples and in a narrow streak from his widow's peak, was always precisely trimmed and controlled with a layer of pomade which held the combed furrows in stern command from the moment of application till he went to bed at night. There was no other barber in town. Uncle Nick cut his own hair, using a mirror, meticulously sharpened scissors, and his long, agile fingers. It took the lubricating effects of serious drinking to loosen Uncle Nick's hair. Then the graying lock at his widow's peak fell forward and down over bleary, repentant eyes. This was the Nick we saw, even through the dry periods and the pomade: befuddled and ridiculous. I remembered the night he scratched at Aunt Anna's window, remembered Gram's name for him: That Nogood SonnaMaBitch. I wondered why he was here. I looked at Josie.

Dad wants to take you someplace, Josie said, grinning her Cheshire Cat grin.

Uncle Nick nodded and smiled, blushing across the pale expanse of his forehead.

I have to make dinner, I said, shifting the groceries from one hip to the other.

What are we having?

Spaghetti and salad. I already made the sauce this morning.

I can do that. Boil spaghetti.

113

Josie stood and took the bag from my arms, peeked in curiously. My arms felt suddenly emptied, my chest vulnerable.

But the salad...

I can do that. You go. Take her, Dad.

Uncle Nick pressed his hands to his knees and rose slowly to his feet. He eased behind me, opened the screen door, and waited in silence. In front of me Josie, balancing my groceries on her hip, blockaded the way to the kitchen.

But you have to do it right, I told her.

She took a long drink from her Coke.

Twelve minutes, Josie. There's an egg timer on the stove. You cook the spaghetti for twelve minutes. You have to listen for the timer. And don't forget to salt the water.

Uncle Nick beckoned patiently from the open doorway.

Not too much salt, either. Just a pinch. Two pinches.

Josie grinned.

Go.

There's lettuce in the shopping bag.

Go.

You could get a tomato and cucumber from the garden. But be sure to wash them with soap.

Uncle Nick beckoned again.

Because of the bomb dust, I explained desperately. *They need to be washed right.*

Josie looked over my head at her father and said, *When you bring her back, Dad, why don't you stay for dinner?*

No. Your mother expects me.

Except when he was too sodden to do anything, Uncle Nick always did what Aunt Anna told him. With a sudden understanding of what that felt like, I threw up my hands and walked out the door.

Shouldn't you be at the shop? I grumbled at Uncle Nick as he opened the front gate for us.

No. I closed early.

The shop was often closed, when Aunt Anna put Uncle

Nick to some task, when he was drinking, when he wandered off. Customers walked in the unlocked shop, took a chair, and waited. Outside, the red-and-white striped pole turned non-committally. The customers left and were replaced by others who waited and left. They would be back. They were used to the vicissitudes of haircuts in Taylor.

We crossed the street and took the shortcut to Main through Mrs. Tatolovich's yard, through her back gate, along the narrow cement path beside her house. From her kitchen sink, Mrs. Tatolovich shook her fist inches from Uncle Nick's ear. From window to window, we watched her progress through the rooms of her house as she moved to intercept us in the front yard. When we rounded the corner of the house, she was waiting on the front porch. She clutched her black sweater in a wrinkled fist and pointed a finger at Uncle Nick. Her babushka nodded; her sharp nose trembled.

This no goddam highway, Meester.

Uncle Nick shrugged helplessly, his neck flaming scarlet as he beat a hasty path to the front gate.

Next time go round, Mrs. Tatolovich waved Uncle Nick away menacingly.

Uncle Nick gently closed the gate behind us and nodded up earnestly at the belligerent, little crow of a woman.

Mala, Mrs. Tatalovich called in a higher, sweeter voice as we crossed Main. *I make sardma. I bring you nice sardma, tomorrow, Mala. You see!*

Thank you, Mrs. Tatalovich, I called over my shoulder.

Uncle Nick leaned over and whispered, *She likes you. That's lucky. She makes the best sardma...*

He waved his hand in a wide arc, encompassing the entire known world.

...don't tell Anna I said so... .

Sardma was a labor-intensive concoction of meat and rice, rolled into sticky balls and wrapped in cabbage leaves, then cooked slowly in sauerkraut and smoked ham hocks and

115

spareribs. When a woman pulled out her secret recipe for sard-ma and started cooking, all of Sixth Street grew fragrant with the smell. Mouths watered uncontrollably for hours. Each recipe was slightly different, considered by its cook the pinnacle of culinary excellence, and carried to the grave in a shroud of undying mystery. In Mrs. Tatolovich's, I detected a hint of dry mustard, and something else, an elusive spice, nutmeg maybe, or allspice.... Aunt Anna floated cloves of garlic in the stewing mixture. Not very inventive, but the meat was succulent after steeping in garlic and sauerkraut all day. As in all things, Aunt Anna expected complete loyalty to her sardma from all her extended family. *The best? Yes, Anna, no question.*

Does Aunt Anna know we're going someplace?

Uncle Nick stopped on the yellow line in the middle of Main Street and blanched.

No.

I could hear a heavy truck rumbling toward town from a long way north.

I won't tell her.

He took my hand and we crossed the street.

Where are we going, Uncle Nick?

Uncle Nick dropped my hand and pointed. Behind town, the cliff caught the late afternoon sun, the narrow trail to the top etching a jagged scar across its glowing face.

To the top?

He nodded as we walked.

Like my mom?

He nodded again.

Really? Did Josie ask you to do it?

No. My idea.

Why?

He stopped and looked down at me.

You asked what she was like. In Anna's kitchen. You asked. We'll go to the top of the cliff, look around, maybe see....

He shrugged. I took his hand and we started walking again.

Next to him, matching my steps to his, I realized that he, too, might be haunted by his mother, might struggle with uncertainty at her fate. Uncle Nick hadn't heard from his mother for twenty years. She was still in a small village outside Zagreb; alive, he and Milan assumed. Every Wednesday, the two brothers gathered at the post office to buy and send off a money order. No note, she could not have read it anyway. The money traveled a thin, worn umbilical cord of love, responsibility, guilt. They had never missed a Wednesday. During the war, Aunt Anna had taken over the duty, scraping together cash, sending it off to a country ripped apart by a vicious invading army and by its own internal hatreds. With each trip to the post office, Aunt Anna shook her head grimly. Still, she did it, for Nick and Milan, for the ritual that meant more than the money.

Do you think she's still alive, Uncle Nick?

He knew immediately whom I was talking about.

The priest will write when she dies, he said, his voice leaden with false certainty.

The truth of the matter was that he didn't know whether his mother, the priest, or even the village existed anymore. Long before the Germans of the last decade, the people fought amongst themselves, like rival packs of dogs, over every scrap of land, every stick and rock, over religion, surname, over battles lost or won a thousand years ago. Over anything. How could one old woman, rejected by her husband, abandoned by her sons, find sanctuary there? I looked up into Uncle Nick's face. His lips moved silently. He was counting his steps, evenly paced prayers, up the steep street that led to the smelter.

Couldn't you have brought her with you?

No. She said she'd never come to America again.

I knew her story, a failed experiment. A bride ordered by mail, then sent back to the Old Country by a brutal, philandering drunk of a husband. But for the two small boys she took back with her, the United States was the country of their birth. They were citizens. Growing up outcasts in their small Serbian village, it had been their only hope.

But, he would have been dead by the time she came back, I said, referring to her husband, Nick and Milan's father. The town called him Dirty Jovo.

Uncle Nick grunted, turned his head aside and spat. Saliva hit the dust in the gutter with a wet slap.

It was a common gesture in Taylor, that stream of precisely placed venom that spoke more loudly than words. From barstools in the dark of the Taylor Club, or from the sun-bleached benches beside the front door, men murmured, hawked, spat. Bartenders complained, *Jesus! I'm going to have to clean that up later!* Nazis, Mussolini, Russians, ancient Turks, bosses up on the hill, a neighbor whose insult has been nursed for a decade, a litany of devils strung together, brought out and expunged with spit. A habit in the blood. Knots of black-clad widows gathered from the length of Sixth Street would laugh and tease, peck and preen, hands in constant, eloquent movement. Then, suddenly something would be said, something remembered. Babuskas electric with fury would turn aside, and in unison the old ladies would spit, raining down curses. Beneath their sturdy black shoes, a condemned soul writhed.

Nick and Milan's dad had been ducking the juices of Taylor for more than fifty years, long before he was shot crawling out of someone else's bedroom window and long before he sent his wife and baby sons back to oblivion in the Old Country. He had been marked for contempt the moment he walked into town, his razor-sharp knife a too-visible bulge beneath his pant leg, his young wife so beaten she was barely recognizable as human. If he had been only a philanderer and a drunk he would have ranked one among many, but he was vicious, filthy, and worst of all, cheap. He only used soap when he was pursuing a new love interest. Then he was smooth and soft-spoken. He mooched off everyone in town and denied his wife the pennies it would take to buy flour and yeast for bread.

She survived from dishes left surreptitiously on the front porch by neighbor women. If he found the food, he kicked the laden plate out into the street and laughed as his wife fought the magpies for scraps. On Sixth Street, Dirty Jovo was low.

When we arrive in Old Country, we have nothing.

Uncle Nick's voice thickened with the accent he had worked so hard to lose. It only resurfaced when he was falling-down drunk or very upset. Like his hair, he controlled each word, speaking little, choosing carefully. That was when Aunt Anna let him talk.

My mother, she say, it don't matter we starve. We already dead of shame.

We had reached the end of Taylor. Except for the road that entered the smelter complex, all the streets running up the hill dead-ended in dirt six feet from the chain link fence. A worn trail ran the perimeter of the fence, as if some creature had circled and circled the smelter. We followed the trail, Uncle Nick leading, then angled off on a less used trail that led toward the smokestack and on to the cliff.

At the cliff, Uncle Nick urged me ahead of him.

I'll make sure you don't fall.

Each step had to be chosen with care, firm rock, not slippery dirt. As Taylor dropped away below me, I felt my confidence grow, my need to climb, to gain the top. My mother's hands grasped each sun-hot rock with me; her feet guided each step. Behind me I heard Uncle Nick grunt and struggle, the slide and scrabble of pebbles cascading below. Halfway up, I stopped on a large outcropping. With my back to the warm cliff I watched Uncle Nick's labored ascent.

My mom came up here a lot?

Uncle Nick nodded, gulping air.

Almost every day about this time, he gasped.

I watched him, his chest heaving, palms braced on knees. He was scanning the town below, his eyes following Avenue C down to Main, then over two blocks along the pale sidewalk to the tiny pole swirling white, red, white, red, over two doors to the Taylor Club with its liquid wealth.

Are we going the rest of the way? I asked gently.

A hank of hair had fallen free, dangling a gray question mark down his forehead and into his left eye. He straightened, licked his dry lips, smoothed his hair back with a sweating hand and, still breathing hard, pointed up.

The top was flat and rocky, a narrow culmination. My legs trembled, both from the climb and the way the world tilted away in front and back.

Clamoring up beside me, Uncle Nick sucked in the thin, high air and looked around. He smiled and kicked the rocky ground with a dusty toe.

Limestone, he puffed. *Good for caves. I'll show you.*

He waved for me to follow him. A short way down the backside of the ridge, stunted pinon and spruce clung to the rock. Through a small thicket of trees no taller than me, the entrance to a cave marked a blacker oblong on the deeply shaded slope.

The snow melts and seeps through the ground. It hollows out the earth. Come on, I'll show you.

Uncle Nick had regained his breath and his hair was back under command. He was master of this surprising subject, a man who knew caves. I followed him curiously. We scrabbled down the slope and through the trees to the entrance. Uncle Nick pulled his battered, silver lighter out of his back pocket and deftly adjusted the tiny wheel on the bottom of the lighter. He flipped the top with his thumb and spun the wheel with one smooth movement. The flame flared four inches high, the smell of butane tickling the air. Holding his thumb to the wheel, he raised his arm. The cave's walls were blacked, the dirt floor charred and strewn with chunks of twisted, blown metal.

Hey! I said excitedly, *This must be the bootlegger's cave!*

Uncle Nick nodded, then sighed, surveying the terrible waste at his feet.

My dad came here to collect it. Gram said it was pretty nasty, but everyone drank it anyway.

Uncle Nick shrugged.

Long time ago. I was over there.

His arm waved off to the east, across one continent, an ocean and halfway across another continent.

There's a better cave. I'll show you.

He let go of the wheel; the flame dropped, disappeared. I followed as he strode further down the slope, to an angled shelf of dirt hidden between two outcropping of rock.

Uncle Nick, how do you know about all this stuff?

I come up here, sometimes. When your mamma died was the first time. I came up here to see...

To see if she jumped? I asked, a quick, sharp bitterness, like crushed limestone, on my tongue. I thought of the bets in the Taylor Club, the rumors that ran like dirty snow melt along the streets of the town.

Uncle Nick shook his head.

No, he said, watching his footing. *To see why she came.*

We were at the mouth of the second cave. Uncle Nick turned to me, his eyes shining, and took my hand.

This is special, he said in a hushed voice.

Sparking the lighter, he held the light high in front of us and drew me gently into the flickering interior.

Watch where you step, he warned.

The floor was scattered with bits of clay pottery. Off to my right, round, smooth stones had been carried up the mountain face from some far river and gathered into a fire ring. Other stones showed the diligently cupped surface of continual grinding.

*Uncle Nick...*I stuttered in amazement.

There's more. Come see this, he whispered and pulled me further back into the cave.

He raised the lighter higher. In the wavering flame, the back wall of the cave swirled and cascaded with movement. Black, fat beasts with bristled horns and narrow, frantic legs streamed across the rough surface. Handprints in deep ochre splashed color in their path. Human figures danced, angular stick bodies splayed ecstatically beneath triangle heads. Waving lines, spirals, arrows, and squares in white, black, and red sprinkled geometry among the scene. An ancient world played. I reached out a tentative hand. Uncle Nick pulled me back, shaking his head.

We can't touch it, he whispered reverently. *Even the light could hurt it.*

We backed away. I took a last look around, knelt by the fire ring, and fingered a slender shard of pottery.

My mom, do you think she knew about this place, Uncle Nick?

He shrugged.

Maybe. Maybe she just stayed on the top. We'll go back up. You'll see.

I placed the shard carefully back into its spot and rose to leave.

You should tell somebody about that cave, Uncle Nick, I said as we climbed back up the east side of the ridge.

I bet people would like to study it. You know. Scientists... or historians or somebody.

The shadows were deeper, the air carrying the cool bite of evening. Uncle Nick stopped and turned to face me.

No. Sometimes, Mala, things are better left to themselves. Sometimes, people look so close at something, they forget what they are seeing. They ruin it.

You must have come up here a lot, to find those caves. Is this where you go when you disappear?

Uncle Nick shrugged, waved vaguely.

Here. There. All over. I don't just go to bars, he explained solemnly. *I just end up there,* he added with a smile, a crooked ghost of Josie's Cheshire grin.

The top of the ridge was washed in slanting, golden rays. Below our feet, Taylor inched through the last of its day. The muted sounds of barking dogs and car engines rose on the cooling air. I could see Gram's house at the edge of the glowing Sands. Josie was making dinner for me, hopefully washing the garden vegetables with a good dose of soap and hot water. Two doors down, Aunt Anna was probably banging her own pots, cursing Uncle Nick, worrying where he was. Standing next to me, he faced east.

Wheeler Peak, he said.

I nodded, not looking, still watching the tiny town at my feet.

Almost at the top of the peak, he said, *there are bristlecone pine trees. Nothing else will grow there, no grass, nothing. The bristlecones like it up there. It's the only place they can live, where nothing else can. Down the mountain, they die. You should see them, Mala. The wind twists them. Hardly any green, don't even look alive. They're the oldest living things. Maybe God made them first. When you touch them, their wood is like marble. They know about surviving.*

These were more words than I had ever heard him string together. I looked over my shoulder at him, the straight back, the dark head with its precise cut. A different man looked east at the pale peak. Gram had been wrong. I had thought she saw into people's hearts, she and all the other old women, saw everything, then condemned or forgave. But, Gram had not known this man. We were all guilty of that.

How do you know all this stuff, Uncle Nick?

He shrugged again.

I look around. I read.

He turned and smiled at me.

Like you, I ask lots of questions.

I looked back down at Taylor, graying in the falling light.

It's ugly.

Not so bad.

You're always leaving.

No. I'm always coming back.

Uncle Nick, do you think she did it? Jumped? Maybe she just couldn't go back down there.

He shook his head.

I don't think about that. That's for her to know...and God. I think about why she came here, he repeated.

He pointed past town, past The Sands, to the deep purple hills at the horizon.

This is what I found.

The flat disk of the sun was just slipping behind the hills. Its angled rays washed the toxic wastes of The Sands in radiant silver, the town in sudden gold. Each feature of land or town etched an ebony shadow, long and leaning, that yearned toward the cliff at my feet. Only the smokestack stood close enough to pencil a thin, black finger on the illuminated face. From the western horizon the color wheel arched above, from the burning orange brilliance of the sinking sun, to rich yellow, deepening to turquoise above me, dropping through blue to purple to a clear, wavering red at the line of the land behind me.

You look this way, too, Uncle Nick urged, gently turning my body to the east. *She did.*

With the dropping light, the contrast between endless mountain ridges and deep valleys flattened, until a single velvet plain of deepest green swept away to the horizon, a different country. There, catching the last escaping rays of sun, Mt. Wheeler's white peak gleamed like a diamond pin fixing land to liquid sky. Too far off to see, stubbornly clinging to the glittering peak, bristlecones lived. Did she know? Would she have listened to their lesson?

Uncle Nick...

Shhh...

Gentle hands squeezed the sharp bones of my shoulders.

Just look.

She had stood here. Nightly, she had stood on this rocky crest and her world had changed beneath her. On one side Taylor, flushed with late gilt, yearning toward her. On the other side, this secret eastern land, smooth and fertile, recognizable to her every atom, a clear and easy path calling her home. She had stood in the twilight between.

Uncle Nick was right. I would never know. She would always be fragments of color splashed across a dark cave wall, fragile, cryptic, open to any interpretation. There was only this place, this apex of her life, this place of departure.

I looked straight up, filled my lungs with air the color of glacial lakes, exhaled ghosts. I floated. If I had raised my arms I would have shot up, gained the surface of the turquoise heavens, soared east or west. It didn't matter. I could have flown.

Now you've seen, Uncle Nick said quietly. *It's getting dark.*

I needed him to go before me this time, to steady my descent. Pebbles showered down on him as I stumbled and slipped, but he only wiped his eyes across his sleeve and silently guided my feet to each firm spot on the trail. It was night when we reached to bottom.

The new sheriff was waiting for us at the top of town. Leaning against the fence, he blocked the narrow path that skirted the smelter. To us he was only an angled shadow, darker than its surroundings. The sudden beam from his flashlight startled and trapped us.

Seen you coming down. A low, sliding voice from darkness.

Caught up like deer in headlamps, Uncle Nick and I were motionless, accepting of this turn in fate.

What you been doing up there with that little girl.

I looked up into Uncle Nick's face, saw the unevenness of his dusty skin in stark incandescence, the evening blur of beard along his jaw line, the hanging lock of hair that carved a dark sickle into his forehead. He blinked, his lashes brushing rapid shadows across his cheeks.

She my niece, he stuttered, his voice foreign. *We take walk. I no do nothing.*

The darkness beyond the beam was thick with disbelief. I heard the sheriff hawk and spit. Beside me, Uncle Nick's head dropped. I inched my hand over and held his.

It's true, I said into the light, added, *I'm not little.*

You are, he said to me.

The flashlight clicked off. Blackness enveloped us. My ears rang in the sudden void. Then the voice, tinged with disgust:

Get the hell outta here. Go on home.

We heard the scrape of a heel further along the path, the rumble of an engine starting at the edge of the street, saw the swing of headlights as the car wheeled around. We stood holding hands, waiting for the night to return to us. Then I led him home.

Uncle Nick, are you okay? I asked as we reached Sixth Street.

He wouldn't answer, couldn't trust himself to arrange the words as they should be. With his free hand he rubbed his chin and mouth. He wetted his lips. His hands trembled.

What you did was good, I soothed, pulling him the last few lengths to Aunt Anna's house.

I opened the front gate and drew him into the yard and up to the door.

Thank you, Uncle Nick.

I hugged him fiercely, briefly. His arms went around me in an automatic way, but his head was turned. He was looking off towards the faint glow of Main Street, the Taylor Club. He was already gone, slipped back into character, chasing a thirst. I opened the door and pushed him gently in. I left him to the rough, capable care of Aunt Anna. I sprinted home to my supper.

15

There would be fireworks. Not the normal 4th of July rockets, erratic and hesitant, that burst like a case of electric hiccups over the Taylor ball field. The Fourth of July was long past. Advertisements stapled to the walls of the market and the post office shouted **BIG FIREWORKS DISPLAY THE FLATS AUGUST 2 COURTESY COPPER KING.**

Courtesy of Copper King, there was the catch. The men of Sixth Street rumbled to each other, *If the Copper King was paying, expect pink slips in pay envelopes come Friday.* The Copper King knew and the men knew it would be harder to complain, to organize and protest if they came home to a wife with the remembered sparkle of fireworks in her eyes.

You'll see, the wives would say to them. *It's just temporary. The pit needs you. The smelter needs you. You'll see.*

The women would pat their men's shoulders and glow down on them the borrowed brilliance of fireworks. The men would stand up in disgust and head to the Taylor Club, pushing through children in the yard who swooped and screamed, fiery missiles of color. The men of Sixth Street were cynical about their employer, but they were usually right. They knew nothing about the price of copper or overseas suppliers. They gauged their future by one thin, green envelope, the pink slip or the grudging, paltry raise it might contain.

Still, there would be fireworks. Wet bottles of beer waited to be rescued from icy baths in tubs carried to the flats in the back of pickups. Young women would pick their way through the sage, their hips swishing in light, soft dresses as they looked for a spot to lay in twos and threes under the stars. Children would sizzle with white-hot joy. And later, maybe, there would be other fireworks, in dark bedrooms with willing wives, women already satiated with the flash and soft drift of light. So the men of Sixth Street put away their grumbling and waited with sly expectation for August 2.

Josie could have gone with her friends. They called, urging her, enticing her with tales of what boys were coming and stolen bottles of liquor.

No, she said. *I'm taking my cousin, Becky. We're having a last fling.*

I knew what that meant. She would be handing me over to Aunt Anna soon. But for Josie that was only a small part of it. The moment the diploma had crossed her palm in June, Josie considered herself a college woman. She had left her classmates in the dust months ago.

She had me take the extra blanket from the hall closet, while she collected a paper bag from under the sink, walked out the back door and down the stairs to the cellar.

Take this, she said, returning and thrusting the full paper bag into my hands. Its ruffled edge was folded and refolded precisely. I could detect glass bottles, cellar-cool through the rough paper. I felt carefully, two Ball jars of Eli's wine.

*If Aunt Anna finds out...*I began.

Josie smiled and raised an eyebrow.

How? she asked with mild curiosity.

My muscles were the first to betray me, tugging at the corners of my mouth. Josie was contagious.

Can Carrie come? I asked.

She took the bag from my hands.

Get her. I'll get another bottle.

If only for a short time, we would be a threesome, each a testament to our mother, linked by a phone call, a secret train ride, a woman wreathed in smoke, a rescue in Uncle Sam's Cadillac, a cliff top. Back together for another escapade. Fireworks.

The town was emptying out as I walked up to Dr. Price's. I dodged cars pulling from driveways and streaming down streets toward Main and out to the flats beyond town. Windows were down, radios blared, children squealed and bounced on

128

back seats. At Dr. Price's the clinic was dark. The lights in the four-bed infirmary were on, Mrs. Escovitich in bed with her gallstones, her unmarried son patient at her side. At the back of the house, kitchen windows glowed gold into the dark shrubbery. I walked around to the back door, knocked on the pane, and waited, looking in on the illuminated scene. Carrie and her father sat washed in light from above the kitchen table. Between them on the table lay two discarded forks, two crumpled paper napkins, two empty glasses, tinged milk-white and a skillet with the remnants of dinner. I didn't need to look to know: scrambled eggs with hotdogs. Carrie came to the door.

Want to come with us to the fireworks? I asked.

Sure. I'll ask.

Carrie returned to her father, leaned low and whispered in his ear. He nodded, and she hugged him quickly, planting a kiss on his temple. She lingered near him a minute and walked away. He watched her back as she came towards me at the door. I thought they must have talked, come to an understanding. In the dark outside, I asked her.

Did you tell him about going to Parker?

Yes.

What did he say?

I got a lecture about jumping the train. Then he wanted to know about her. He was so...I don't know...eager. Her voice was sad, old.

What did you tell him?

Just what she said... .

Karina, I thought and imagined scarlet lips forming the word. The sound was a whisper, a sigh of silken sheets.

He said sometimes people don't know who they are or what they want. It takes time. They make mistakes.

I considered the words as we walked down the hill. They seemed to hang in time. Did they refer to when he had met her, wooed her, unknowing? Did they explain for him why she left? Why he followed, why he stayed? What he was waiting for?

129

Did it explain the woman and her distilled offering, that one word, her child's name? Perhaps the words were only a balm, an ointment from the row of bottles on Dr. Price's shelves, gently soothing symptoms of disease, but missing the cure. People slipped, fell, couldn't always be saved.

I don't understand, I said, shaking my head. *What will happen now?*

He made me promise not to go back, she said finally. *I promised. That's all.*

Promises were cottonwood seed, fluid and shifting like dreams, sometimes lost, sometimes lodging, bearing fruit. Children.

Over here!

Josie grinned like a beacon from across Main, juggling blanket and bag of clinking bottles.

Cokes? Carrie asked.

Eli's wine, I said in a low voice.

She took the bag from Josie, unfolded it and peeked in.

One for each. Wow.

She carefully refolded the bag, tucked it under her arm, and allowed herself a wide, pleased smile. It was almost like a smile I remembered on the face of a girl, reckless and unknowing, who had once leaned over an open grave to charm a blush from a boy. Josie flagged a late-leaving pickup as it passed. Old Man Papich waved from behind the wheel, stopped just long enough for us to jump into the back. The gears ground; the truck lurched forward. Between our feet, a zinc tub sloshed ice water, bottles rattled a muted complaint.

We're not the only ones planning a party tonight, Josie commented.

She turned to grin into the wind. Her hair whipped back from her face, a flowing, snapping banner. We swung past two sedans in sedate procession. The interior bristled in black. The collected members of the widow's club jostled for space, heavy black purses clutched to ample breasts. I waved gaily into the receding headlights.

What do they think they're going to do with those purses? Carrie hollered.

Hand out fifty-cent pieces to kids and clobber drunken men, I hollered back.

Old Man Papich dropped us off next to a clutch of family cars.

Aunt Anna presided over the gathering: sisters, sisters-in-law, a collection of dark-haired offspring. The men of the family had already inched off to cluster around tailgates a safe distance from Anna. Uncle Nick was not there. He had slipped away again. But, like he said, he was always coming back. Anna would be waiting from him, ready to dust him off, sober him up, set him to work. Queen bee of every family event, she stood in the center of the milling crowd of relations, orchestrating activities, sending out her drones to do her bidding.

Where is Sam? Evie, go get that husband of yours. They shouldn't be drinking before they have some cake in their stomachs. Where's Emil? Kiki, cut more cake than that...

I'll do the talking, Josie warned us as we maneuvered around the edges of the family.

There you are! Aunt Anna pounced. *Josie, where's your accordion? I told you to bring it! Mala, help Kiki with the cake.*

Aunts Kiki and Mimi quivered near a huge chocolate sheet cake. They waved at us minutely.

Look, Kiki. It's Josie and Mala. And a little friend.

Becky, Mimi, Aunt Kiki whispered and peeked over at Aunt Anna.

The little friend is Becky? Mimi blinked and offered a hand.

No, Mimi dear. Mala is Becky. Remember? Josie says so....

Kiki took Mimi's dangling hand and gave it a gentle squeeze.

Oh yes, you're right, Kiki. Becky.

Josie deftly draped Gram's blanket over the paper bag and

began working her way through sage and bodies. I hugged Aunt Kiki, kissed Mimi's cheek, and slipped passed them. Carrie followed closely.

Who is the little friend? Mimi worried at the empty air.

You come back here! Aunt Anna commanded us. *Where are you going?*

Plans, Ma, Josie waved vaguely toward a distance point.

You do as I say! You stay with your family!

Josie shook her head; we hid ours and kept moving. From behind us, Aunt Anna's voice cut like a knife through the awed silence.

For crying out loud. Kiki, don't cut the cake like that. I'll do it. Little Pauly don't slurp that soda. Mimi, find a place and sit!

We threaded our way through a dark patchwork of blankets, brush, running children, yelling mothers, trucks parked haphazardly and surrounded by men who laughed low and talked about their chances of having a job next week. Beer bottles clinked. Standing among the men somewhere would be Naked Sal, his dirty bare shoulders rubbing ones hung in faded cotton. He would listen to their talk, smile, nod vacantly. He might venture to tell them the recipe for combustible rockets, might cite the history of the firework. The men would laugh and slap his back, moderating their blows to land with a gentle thud. The Methodist-Minister-Without-a-Flock would stand at Sal's elbow, drinking as quickly as possible, interpreting Sal's raveled memories for the crowd.

What my friend means, gentlemen, what he means is…is…it's going to be a fine show!

Somewhere nearby, Naked Sal's sister, Miss Amelia, would hover watchful as a mamma bird, waiting for a chance to swoop down, force legs through trousers, arms through a light jacket.

We moved on into the neatly arranged spread of up-towners. Unlike the rowdy miner's families, the families from above Main remained intact on their blankets, the fathers patient and quiet, the mothers yoohooing and waving to each other while ever-watchful of their children, monitoring who they played with and how.

We chose a spot away and slightly uphill from the rest. Carrie and I spread the blanket, hoping no rattlesnakes lay silent and invisible in the speckled, moonlit dirt. Josie passed around the pint bottles. We each struggled with the wide-mouthed lids for a moment, were rewarded with the satisfying low pop as they gave way beneath our might. We stood ceremoniously on our blanket and raised our bottles up to the sky, ringing them together.

Freedom, Josie called into the night.

Among the three of us, only Josie was sharp enough to cut all the strings and float free. Carrie and I exchanged a glance, then obliged Josie with a long, slow drink to her freedom. We didn't want freedom. We wanted attachment. The wine was thick and sweet in our throats. We breathed in the diminishing warmth of the earth and stood watching darkness settle down on our collected townsmen. Hundreds of cigarettes glowed and winked. At the edge of the crowd, the volunteer firefighters milled around their tank truck ready to rush off to any hot spot, their yellow rubber jackets flashing in the truck's parking lights. A single beam of light worked its way through the crowd. I pointed. Lit by his flashlight, the new sheriff moved through the crowd with his loose-limbed, predator's gait. The flashlight swung with deceptive, casual grace, then suddenly zeroed a bull's eye of white light on a startled, frightened face. I shivered.

He won't come up here. There's no one to scare, Josie said, her voice laced with a distant contempt.

Far off to the east, beyond The Sands and the distant hills, sheet lightning awakened the sky intermittently. A breeze carried the tangy promise of a summer storm. Two sets of car lights crept from the highway and swung out into the quieting crowd. The widows had arrived. We were complete. Now there would be fireworks.

Backs on the scratchy wool blanket, we looked straight up, hushed and waiting, sipping from carefully angled jars. The stars swam in the warm glow of wine.

A sudden boom, a streak of smoke, a crack, the sky exploded in shimmering red. In quick succession, two more booms, two cracks, blue, white. Josie whooped. Carrie laughed with delight, tears sparking the corners of her eyes. The sky was filled with chrysanthemums of light, dazzling petals drifting lazily down upon us. From below us, the oohs and ahhs of hundreds of mothers and children floated up to meet the cascade of light. Aunt Anna's voice arced above the crowd, pierced the heavens.

Another! she demanded.

Boom! Crack!

Josie leapt to her feet and danced, arms flung wide, spinning among falling stars, then dropped to the blanket exhausted, thrilled.

Another! Anna called out.

Boom! Crack!

The mingled voices of women and children, the cheers of men, the smack of half-empty beer bottles raised and saluting. I imagined Dr. Price off in Taylor sitting quietly beside Mrs. Escovitich, her gallstones, and her son. They stilled at the distant noise and smiled. On some barstool or some mountaintop, maybe, Uncle Nick paused, feeling the short, sharp pull of home. We were all of us joined at last in that moment of bliss, fleeting as fireworks. Thousands of hopes distilled then set loose in a brilliant explosion that ruptured the darkness. Birth. The fuel and fumes of mothers, I thought, a country of mothers.

What do they all want? I asked, watching the stars fight for purchase in the smoke-washed blackness between bursts.

Josie laughed.

Who?

She thought it was the wine talking.

People, I said. *Everyone...*I hesitated *...mothers....*

Boom! Crack! Ahhh!

Mothers? That's easy! Josie shouted. *They want to tell us what to do!*

No, Carrie said her voice softly slurred, quiet in the glittering air. *No, Josie. They want us to not be like them.*

Josie laughed again, a sound like a bubbling spring in the desert.

You two are drunk!

Perhaps it was the wine. I know the voices of my cousin and my friend, the chorus of the town, buoyed me. The stars came down to meet me. The darkness was filled with splashes of color, wings of light, stories, dreams, promises.

No, I told them. *They want us to fly.*

Part 3

16

Naked Sal had his first bath in thirty years on a Wednesday in late August. The air was hot and heavy, a perfect day for public bathing, if you were of the mind. Sal had not been of that mind for a very long time.

The slight wind from the east carried an expectant sizzle. Mammoth white clouds with bruised-looking undersides gathered over the western hills beyond The Sands. On Main Street, wives and widows gathered in tight knots along the sidewalk, bright summer cottons mingling with perennial black wool. There was a tension to their postures, heads tilted forward, eyes furtive. Morning shopping had been forgotten for the moment. Here, too, a storm was brewing.

It was the eighth day since Copper King had begun layoffs. Men who should have been up at the smelter or over in the pit beyond Parker were home in bed or sitting morosely at kitchen tables. They were in the way. At night, the men came home from the Taylor Club and the pool hall too early, disrupting the radio-listening schedule. That new sheriff was on the prowl. He stood in the doors of the bar and then walked among the tables, noting faces. He never talked to the men. He never drank with them. He watched. Cowed, the miners came home to Sixth Street edgy and mostly sober. They yelled at their wives and slapped their kids and then blamed it on the company and the new sheriff. It was getting so a man couldn't get a simple drink in his own town, the men complained to their wives.

It's not your town, the women told them. It's the company's town and the new sheriff's, the women said, so you'd better behave. Their voices were matter-of-fact, but underneath the women seethed, feared, their words echoing in their chests, *not your town,* and these unspoken words, too ...*not ours.* In front yards or at the doors of Main Street stores the women collected, raining down anger and worry. Listening to their daughters and neighbors, the black-clad widows nodded gray heads, incensed, too, with this change in the natural order. To the general lament they added their own particular complaint.

He no Sheriff Billy, they moaned. *This one no respect.*

The new sheriff called the widows by their first names. Never since they were girls in their mother's houses had they been called by their first names. They had been called You, Woman, Old Woman, Mama, Grammama, Missus and plenty of names by their late husbands that they repeated with lip-smacking relish and not a single blush.

This naming was different. When the new sheriff walked through their little street side gatherings, he tipped his hat solemnly, looked them each in the eye and said, *Morning, Dorothy, Martha, Jane.*

It wasn't even their real names. He used the Americanized version typed by some clerk on paper that later this man, this stranger, read and used to mark them. *You are Jane, not Janitsa, now,* his simple greeting said. *You are in my country now.*

It brought them back to the first moment they stepped on this land, immigrants. Here by the grace of men like him, not, as they had thought, by their own hard work. When the new sheriff walked through them, they dropped their eyes and scattered like birds caught tasting the farmer's corn. He made them feel small.

No like 'em. I say nogood sonamabitch.

But the condemnation was muttered covertly, with a hushed tone that echoed the quiet, far-off mutter of thunder in the west.

Shhh, was the hissed warning. *Careful...best say nothing.*

A quick, sharp gesture from a gray head and the urgent whisper, *Look, coming!*

Into this electric atmosphere the new sheriff came, tall, narrow and hard. He dragged Naked Sal down the sidewalk. The new sheriff had found him hiding under the bleachers at the ballpark. Naked Sal was blubbering incoherently, the sound a long exhalation of despair. Face invisible beneath his fedora, the sheriff carried the look of a man fed up. The worn-down heels of his cowboy boots punched the sidewalk angrily. His knuckles were white where they grasped Naked Sal around the biceps and pulled him along. The two of them went through the front of the Sheriff's Office with a snap of its spring door. The sound of the cell door clanging shut rang along the street. Merchants and customers came out of shops and stood looking around, wondering. The knots of women on the street stood transfixed. The new sheriff came out of his office with another slap of the screen door, and from beneath his fedora, surveyed the street and wiped Sal's transferred filth from his hands to the front of his faded red shirt.

It was Naked Sal's twelfth time behind bars, for Vagrancy, Indecency, Public Nuisance, Lewdness. Naked Sal should have been familiar with all the terms. He was Taylor's first, last and only lawyer. Naked Sal had been to college a long time ago. It was a fine old college, too, in the East with stone buildings clothed in ivy and green lawns that stretched to blue still waters, according to his sister, Miss Amelia. He had gone to law school, and then had moved West, hired by the Bureau of Indian Affairs. He had helped to settle a grazing dispute in Wyoming before he moved on to Nevada to work on a water rights dispute brewing between the native Piute Indians and a group of ranchers outside a tiny mining community called Taylor. With Miss Amelia, Sal rented a company house two doors off Main on A Street and set about taking depositions, traveling to the reservation in the hills on the other side of The Sands, and tracking down old treaties and deeds in the basement of the county courthouse. Taylor was very proud of its new addition, a big-shot eastern lawyer.

Then one day, walking out of county court into the cool

evening air of Parker, three ranchers hefting two-by-fours settled the water dispute forever. Sal was in a coma for five months. Miss Amelia sat by his bed with a Colt .45 resting in her dainty lap and her hands constantly busy tolling off Our Fathers and Hail Marys on her great-grandmother's pink quartz rosary beads. She was sure the miscreants would return to finish off her beloved brother. Both she and God would be waiting. Sal woke up one evening, and in a voice cracked with disuse recited the Declaration of Independence, a good part of the Constitution of the United States, the Hippocratic Oath, and Newton's Laws. After a short pause to rest his aching vocal chords, he announced to his gladdened, bewildered sister, *I shall go naked into this world!* And he did.

Sal would never be a lawyer again. If his lack of clothing hadn't barred him from the courtroom, his mental state would have. All the slender filaments that connected a human to rational forward movement through life had been tangled. With their two-by-fours, the ranchers had stirred Sal's brains into a great stew of high emotions and extreme confusion. In the mixing process, however, every bit of errant information Sal had ever learned or heard had bubbled to the surface, unbidden. With a little patience and prompting, he could be relied on to know anything—well, anything a person in Taylor needed to know. For the past three decades, he had written nearly every high school report in Taylor. Two bits and a smile yielded at least four pages smeared and dirty, closely printed in shaky pencil, from the Dred Scott Decision to Aristotle to the mysteries of the periodic chart or a novel by Dickens. A perfect *A* every time. In between writing assignments, Sal cultivated his nakedness, acquired layers of sun and dirt, hardened his extremities against cold, heat, and the sting of blowing sand and dust. He grew crafty in avoiding Miss Amelia, who prayed to the watchful eye of the Virgin, hunted him down and gathered him home on deadly cold nights, and never gave up trying to clothe her brother in the sight of God. He became the darling of every man and woman down on Sixth Street, though he was not so welcome above Main.

To the men and women of Sixth Street, Naked Sal was clothed in higher education, something they had never worn. He had their unconquerable respect. At the Taylor Club, he was treated to beers by men who listened to his spasmodic explosions of knowledge with absorption and an eye to self-improvement, monitoring his intake of alcohol while disregarding their own. They knew this: coming home to Sixth Street drunk was one thing, but coming home to face a wife or mother who knew through some mysterious female telepathy that Naked Sal was inebriated was more than the enjoyment of seeing his dirty face glowing joyfully drunk could ever be worth. If Sal chose, he could be nude, filthy, stinky, and nuts, that was all fine, but if the women of Sixth Street could help it, he would never be drunk like a common man, like their husbands. The women of Sixth Street coaxed Naked Sal into their homes, fed and warmed him, and continually renewed his mantle of dignity by their reverence. For thirty years he had been their cause, their child. They had done a good job. Sheriff Billy had let them, respecting their need to nurture as he did Sal's need to nakedness. He had let them be.

From the deep shade of his hat, the new sheriff eyed the stilled crowd along Main Street and then turned on his rounded heels and disappeared along the side of the building into the alley behind. He came back kicking a huge whiskey barrel before him and with a coiled hose over his shoulder. The barrel rolled with an aching, hollow sound punctuated by the penetrating thump of the new sheriff's boot. The new sheriff upended the barrel on the sidewalk in front of his office. Dropping one end of the hose into the barrel, he worked his way back into his office, uncoiling the rope as he went. The sound of water erupted in the wooden barrel. The sheriff emerged with a new scrub brush and a blue bar of Boraxo, laid them on the bench by the front door, and stood watching the barrel fill. Rooted to their spots, the crowd listened to the sound of the filling barrel, a slight chill rising in their legs as if they stood in the deepening water. At last, the sheriff walked back into his office and the water stopped. In the hushed street the sound of the cell door swinging back on its hinges was heard and after three quick beats of the watchers' hearts, Naked Sal was thrust blinking and with a silly grin of hope into the harsh light of the day.

Get in.

The new sheriff's voice was low, but clear to everyone the length of the street. There was a scattered, short-lived clapping from one merchant and two uptown ladies. The smile drooped from Sal's face as he stood with his belly pressed against the cold whiskey barrel. He looked around uncertainly, beseechingly, and then down into the water.

Get in.

Sal whimpered, his whole body trembled, but slowly, slowly he raised himself on the edge of the barrel and dropped in. A visible shiver ran through him as the cold mountain water closed around him. He kept his arms up high and teetered on his tiptoes. The lip of the barrel came up to his navel. Already, as he swayed and balanced, a thin circlet of brownish-pink skin showed cleanly between the water and the caked, offending dirt.

Down.

Sal hesitated, searching for meaning in the new sheriff's words. Without speaking further, the new sheriff thrust Naked Sal's head beneath the water. Sal came up sputtering. The new sheriff applied soap and brush. Sal filled his lungs and called out in a pleading, explanatory voice to the people in the street,

The use of light and reflection in Dickens' novel is meant to signify the superficial, transitory nature of—

The new sheriff thrust him under again. Sal came up hacking. The brush and soap were applied again and Sal squawked,

Darwin's Theory of Evolution clearly states—

Down again. This time longer. Sal surfaced and gasped weakly,

We hold these tru—

Down.

You goddam idiot, the new sheriff said in a quiet, hard voice punctuated by his whole body, the straining hands that pushed Sal's head down, the braced legs, the stiff back, the arms locked straight, keeping Sal under. All along the street, men and women held their breath, counted.

Sal came up, silently this time, body heaving, shivering. The sheriff hauled him bodily from the water and dropped him like a crumpled paper cup onto the sidewalk. Sal lay on the warm cement, his body still and curled like a newborn.

Get up.

Sal pulled erect and stood, legs trembling beneath him. Along the street, every eye, except the new sheriff's, dropped.

Now go get dressed.

The new sheriff turned his head. Beneath the brim of his hat, his eyes watched the clouds stacked up above the far hills. His wet shirt clung to the bars of his ribs, the faded fabric deeply red, renewed. With a shove of his booted foot, the new sheriff sent the barrel splashing into the gutter. Thirty years of carefully tended grime and dignity swirled in a gray-brown wash down the hot gutter toward the sewer drain.

Sal, scoured and utterly, utterly naked, ran.

17

There is a sound I remember. Once, when I was six, on one of those trips in which Aunt Anna whisked Gram and me west to visit my two uncles, we were driving through a high, wide valley of sagebrush and tufts of cheat grass. We must have been about twenty miles from Austin, two hundred miles left to go till Reno. The car seat was blistering hot and we raced along with all the windows wide open. The air roared through the back seat, tugging loose single hairs from Gram's and my matching braided buns and flinging them in our blinking eyes. As we moved deeper into the valley, the teasing wind brought us an eerie noise, at first low and broken, but soon rising and insistent, a sound as if the earth itself were keening. Off in front of us, a lone figure stood beside the road, barely recognizable in the hovering heat waves.

Aunt Anna muttered, *What the hell?...* as we moved toward it, riding, it seemed, on the wind and the cry.

Through the dissipating mirage, a cow became visible. She stood over a bloodied, tangled lump, a calf, killed by one of the cars that raced through that stretch of Highway 50.

Jesus. Why can't they fence this highway!

Aunt Anna slowed to forty-five and pulled over into the opposite lane. She was unsure what despairing cattle did under such circumstances. Perhaps the cow would throw herself in front of the car, preferring to join her child; perhaps she would attack the metal beast on behalf of the child that could not protect itself. Aunt Anna was wary. She knew what she would have done. Attacked.

The cow ignored us. Her hooves planted to either side of her still calf, her neck arched back and her muzzle strained up to the flat, blue sky, standing sentinel, she bellowed her affliction, a raging, aching song of loss.

Don't look!

Aunt Anna stepped on the gas. We looked, and Gram, recognizing, crossed herself, a prayer for a fellow mother who had lost a child. She reached for me and pulled me tight against her, determined by sheer force to save this last little one.

I remember the sweating, soft, dough-scented bulk of her bosom, her hot, sun-drenched shoulder against my cheek. I remember looking back, holding the punishing hair from my eyes. I watched the mother cow, I listened to her mournful lowing until both vision and sound disappeared into the obscuring mirage.

On the Thursday morning after Naked Sal's Bath, I was outside checking for storm damage, barefoot among Gram's tomatoes and peas. The sound brought me to my feet, held me in a lost memory, shaking in the wet grass. It was endless, deep and quick with pain. It traveled along the early morning streets of the town, reaching into open windows, bringing heads up sharply from cups of coffee and making those still sleeping twist and burrow into their pillows. The cottonwood leaves rustled with its touch, and the dogs in town joined in mournful canon.

Josie came onto the porch in her nightgown, hairbrush in hand.

What is that?

Something terrible, I whispered.

Josie stepped from the porch, brushed the broken vines from my fingers and pulled me through the front gate. All down Sixth Street, people were stepping out of houses and walking into the street. Half dressed, half shaven, in slippers and barefoot, we crossed through side yards without a complaint from the owners. From uptown, people in much the same state of undress joined our mass and we proceeded down the middle of Main, following the sound.

Across from the post office there was a small town park. A stretch of grass with a never-used bandstand and a single ancient cottonwood was all there was to Taylor Town Park Courtesy Of Copper King. Stray dogs liked it, and for much the same reason some of the patrons of the Taylor Club did too, angling drunkenly across the street late at night to relieve themselves against the tree before performing a precarious right-face and heading back or home.

Naked Sal had used the tree, too, some time the previous night. Knowing exactly where to place the knot along the circumference of his neck, he had hanged himself from the thickest of the lower limbs with a length of white rope. Miss Amelia stood before him, arms at her side, head thrown back, keening. It was she who had called us. Keeping a distance, the crowd gathered around Miss Amelia, the tree, the dead man. Even as we filled the grass and the bandstand and spilled out into Main and D Streets she wailed, a terrible, lost, animal sound.

At last, her voice dropped to a ragged moaning. Miss Amelia turned and reached out her arms, imploring us.

Don't look! I didn't dress him... I didn't make him wear those clothes. He asked for them. He asked! Please...please...don't look at him....

We couldn't help it. We had to see.

Naked Sal had been a bigger man when he last wore the clothes. The cuffs of his white shirt and gray pinstriped jacket hung down his hands so that only the pink tips of his scrubbed fingers peeked out. The waist of his suit trousers was too wide, and even with a belt, dipped from his hips forward, showing a sad separation of shirttails, the blue-and-white band of briefs, and a tender triangle of tanned, cleaned belly. His shoes had slipped from his unresisting feet and dropped with perfect uniformity onto the ground beneath him. During the night the storm had washed him again. Water dripped from one white sock and landed with a plop in his right shoe, spreading small ripples in the small pool of water caught within. His clothes, in thick wet strips, clung to his body, as if at last they had found purchase and would never let go.

146

Please. Please, Miss Amelia moaned and tried to shield Sal from the crowd.

He doesn't want you to see him like this. Not like this... .

So, George Pappas shinnied up the tree, and inching along the limb, pulled a switchblade from his back pocket and cut Sal down. My Uncle Stan and Nick Savich caught him as he dropped, straight and heavy as ripe fruit into their hands. His head fell back on his broken neck as the men carried him. His eyelids slid open. His vision absorbed into the sun and the empty blue sky, Sal passed down the street toward Simple's Funeral Home, unseeing. Mouthing soundless novenas, Miss Amelia picked up his shoes, emptied the water, and followed, shoes clutched to her thin chest, the wet leather soles imprinting a dark pattern on her pale blue housedress. Sal traveled through the parting, silent people, past the new sheriff, who stood at the edge of the crowd bareheaded and unshaved, his young son's hand held in his. The townspeople, in nightgowns or undershirts, barelegged, tousle-headed, bare feet dirty from the streets, turned and walked behind. This was the first of Sal's funeral processions. In his gray suit and white shirt, his shiny belt buckle and dripping white socks, even accessorized as he was in his white rope tie, Sal was the most completely and best dressed person in Taylor that morning.

18

The Howl woke Udiah Simple, too. He listened, then scented the air carried on the long, hollow note of despair. Udiah Simple smelled death and business. Worried that time was short, he rose, put on his dark brown bathrobe, and went out onto the front porch of the funeral home. His maroon pajama bottoms pooled around his white feet. Insensible to the cold boards of the porch, he watched the street and waited. He had been right. It wasn't long. When the body arrived in the arms of George, Nick, and my Uncle Stan, Udiah Simple threw open the double front doors and gestured the party onto the porch.

*The deceased...*he whispered, peeking over Nick Savich's shoulder. No surprise showed on his face as he marked the rope tie and its owner.

...and the bereaved... .

He bent low over Miss Amelia, tried to take one of her hands, to press it in moist condolence. Miss Amelia's stone fingers clutched Sal's shoes, unrelenting. Pulling himself up straight with a supple uncoiling of his back, Udiah smoothed back the greasy hank of hair that had fallen over his eyes as he had bowed.

I am at your service, he said coolly. *Please step this way.*

Sal was carried inside and laid out on the steel embalming table. In the back room Udiah Simple seemed to grow, filling out his pajamas, making his robe billow and ripple.

Gentlemen, Madam, go now, he gestured. *Let me do my work.*

He put his hands out to Miss Amelia.

I'll take those shoes.

When Miss Amelia didn't respond, he attempted to pry Sal's oxfords from her arms.

I think she wants the shoes, George Pappas observed. His words held a slight, sharp edge.

148

It seems so, Udiah relented, annoyed.

I do have spares, he said thinly smiling, waving toward a closed door at the far side of the room. *I'm fully stocked, completely prepared. Ready to go at a moment's notice.*

He ushered the men and Miss Amelia, still cradling Sal's shoes to her chest, out through the parlor and onto the porch.

At the base of the steps the whole town waited. Udiah Simple, on stage, opened his arms. His robe and pajama sleeves fell back, revealing blue veins on thin arms. He raised his voice.

Don't worry, Miss Amelia. The Dearly Departed is in capable hands. Just let me do my work. He'll look wonderful. He'll look very natural. Very natural.

Nick Savich and my uncle carefully eased the catatonic Miss Amelia, with her burden of shoes, down the stairs. A throng of old women in nightgowns and scratchy black sweaters, their hair still in pin curls or last night's braids, their hands still floured from making morning bread, engulfed her and gently swept her home. The crowd fractured and scattered. Shocked and heartsick, all of Sixth Street slipped silently back home to the troubled comfort of cooling loaves of bread and boiled-over coffee.

George, Nick and Uncle Stan stood alone in a loose knot at the base of Udiah Simple's porch stairs, the weight of their burden still in their arms.

*Very natural...*murmured Nick Savich sadly, rubbing the flat of his palm over his stubbly chin.

Verrry natural, George Pappas echoed, mimicking Udiah Simple's high, nasal whine, and kicked the bottom step viciously.

Uncle Stan raised his head slowly, looked into the two men's faces, and smiled.

In the back room of the funeral parlor, Udiah Simple, now dressed in a dark suit and green coverall, stripped the wet, clinging clothes from Sal and stood back, smiling slightly. He was relieved to see that the stories he had heard about the previous day were true. He would not have to wash the body. But the clothes would certainly have to go; they were too large and out of date, and if nothing else, one simply didn't wear white socks to one's own funeral. Striding to his work closet, he rifled through layers of trousers, shirts, and jackets, occasionally glancing over his shoulder at Sal, naked and motionless on the steel table. He ran his fingers over the textures of wool and cotton and sniffed their dry, pleasant fragrance. Those white curls of Sal's would look nice with a blue suit, or dove gray, maybe, Udiah thought. Blue tie, white shirt, dark blue socks, about a size eight shoe, black. He thought of Miss Amelia's grip on the dead man's shoes. A flush rose on his bluish neck. He would charge extra for the shoes, he decided. Udiah carried the clothes over and laid them lovingly on his desk, smoothed the folds and returned to the body on the table. Udiah shook his head at the body's remarkable, all-over tan. A pity he wouldn't need makeup. Udiah loved the feel of the brushes and tiny pots of tint in his hands. Still, a little blush for the cheeks and forehead, a little crimson #6 for the lips, and of course that neck would need some real help. He nodded as he pulled on thick, red rubber gloves. Strapping Sal down securely at knees and belly and shoulders, Udiah Simple went to work.

It didn't start out as Sal's wake. Aunt Anna had gathered the family for a kind of Last Supper. Uncle Mike was moving to Battle Mountain in search of a job, Aunt Millie to Reno. A farewell party for the rest of us, for Anna it was a last chance to argue her brother and sister and their families into staying on Sixth Street where they belonged. No one mentioned celebrating Josie's going to college in two weeks; no one dared.

Out back by Anna's garage, the men had gathered around a fire pit. They drank from long-necked beer bottles and watched the juices from a spitted lamb drip and sizzle in a makeshift tin trough nestled in the red and gray coals. With the toes of their boots they silently prodded the ends of logs deeper into the blaze and listened to Paul and Josie, pressed into service by their mom, play Serb standards on the guitar and accordion.

Inside, the women quietly worked, assaulted by Aunt Anna's complaints and Sofie's dutiful, never-ending rendition of "Beautiful Dreamer" on an old piano rolled down to the house from the Taylor Club.

Everyone is leaving, Aunt Anna viciously accused her steaming pot of sauerkraut.

Why? There's no reason. Copper King will bring the jobs back.

She was met with a face full of steam and bubbling doubt.

This is home, she said, waving her ladle threateningly around the room.

From the women, a few frightened nods as they ducked their heads and set to their tasks, slicing bread, arranging cookies, tearing lettuce.

They'll come back, she assured the boiling pot.

Strains of "Beautiful Dreamer" argued with her from the other room. Middle C sounded flat.

This town, this street is home.

The sound of the music and the scent of the roasting lamb filtering from Anna's home brought them. No one on Sixth Street could resist a potential party. Showing up by two and three, bringing partial loaves of bread, quickly thrown-together salads, jugs of wine and six-packs of beer and pop, everyone came. The house and yard slowly swelled with people, impromptu games of tag and kick the can materialized among the kids. Only the widows weren't there. The widows were at Miss Amelia's, cleaning her already clean house, cooking a month's worth of meals to be stacked in the deep-freeze, gently easing her grief with myriad questions and commands.

Everyone talked quietly about the families that were leaving and the ones already gone. They talked about the Copper King and the coming winter. No one mentioned Sal. The long, pointing shadow his hanging body had cut in the early morning sun still darkened our vision. Each man and woman held a portion of sadness and guilt, heavy and bitter at the back of the tongue, making it hard to swallow. Only the wine, the beer, the whisky and vodka flowed smoothly. They blinked down at their full plates and acknowledged each to himself: *We are not as strong as we thought.* It wasn't much of a celebration.

Uncle Stan, George Pappas, and Nick Savich arrived late. They walked down the side lawn toward the glowing embers with their arms slung around each other's shoulders, their white teeth grinning in the darkness. Men waved them toward the fire, women urged them to eat, but Stan, George, and Nick, proudly slopped against each other, stopped at the edge of the crowd and stood grinning until they had won the attention of every person in the yard.

Everybody, Uncle Stan boomed in a voice like an announcer at a boxing ring. *Everybody, Sal has been returned to that state he so much enjoyed.*

In the stunned, sharp pause the fire crackled and sparks flew upward into darkness. The air held the weight of birth. Uncle Stan waited for us to collect ourselves before he started his story.

We were still up at Simple's Funeral Parlor, hanging around and feeling pretty bad.

Yep, pretty bad... George Pappas intoned.

It occurred to us...occurred to us that Sal might object to some of his funeral arrangements...if he was in a condition to do so.

The night was thick with listening, the crackling of pinon logs unnaturally loud in the waiting air. Aunt Anna came out of the back porch wiping her hands on a dishtowel. The door banged and everyone jumped.

What's going on out here? Why isn't anybody eating? Eat! Eat!

Shhh, Anna, someone urged from the dark. *Stan's here. He's telling us something.*

Stan! Where the hell have you been? Everything's cold! Get a plate, get some—

Shhh!, the whole crowd together.

Aunt Anna froze on the third step, her affront boiling down on us.

Uncle Stan continued, *We decided to have a little talk with Mr. Udiah Simple.*

We leaned toward the smiling trio, willing the story from them.

Just get his opinion on a few matters, Nick Savich added.

*Make a few suggestions...*offered George.

He agreed with us.

We gasped.

In the end...

There was a broad flash of white teeth.

What!? What?! the crowd urged.

Sal's naked, Uncle Stan said simply.

He's Naked Sal! Nick Savich erupted triumphantly.

He'll look verry natural, added George Pappas in a high, nasal whine familiar to everyone present.

Slowly, one by one, startled, tentative grins appear in the dancing firelight. A loud, jubilant war cry sounded somewhere near the third step down from the back porch, and Aunt Anna flung herself down the stairs and hugged the three laughing men.

Now eat! she commanded. *Everybody eat!*

The party began at last. There were a hundred questions thrown at the men. The answers were few, sly, and evasive, but a picture finally arose. It seemed the discussion Stan, George, and Nick had with Mr. Simple was filled with factual anecdotes about the county. They described for him the dimensions of the copper pit, lingering on its depth, the steepness of its sides, how long it took a man falling, bouncing, rolling to reach the bottom. They described the numerous prospectors' mines they had found while hunting. Lost, lonely mines. Bottomless. Nick asked Udiah if he was a hunting man. No, Udiah wasn't. Well, he'd have to learn, they all agreed. They'd be glad to take him out. This brought forth the topic of terrible hunting accidents and then just hideous accidents in general. Here was a conversation Udiah could join. He had dealt with the by-products of discharged guns, chance meeting with mountain lions and rattlesnakes, car crashes on Highway 50. However, Uncle Stan noted, Mr. Simple's usual relish in the subject was lacking.

You threatened him! Aunt Anna burst in. It was hard to tell in the dark whether she was filled more with pride or outrage.

I wouldn't say that... murmured Nick Savich.

He seemed pretty agreeable to me, added George.

Anna's just mad because she didn't think of it first, Uncle Stan's teeth flashed.

No one dared laugh. Aunt Anna went back to commanding everyone, *Eat!* To Paul and Josie, *Play! Play!*

It was a small victory, too late for Naked Sal, but we held it aloft and admired it, the brave, pirate-hearted men, the cowering Simple. In the dark that night, we awarded it the echo of legend and sent it toward the stars amid smoke and sparks from the fire. I wished Gram could have been there with us, and my friends, the widows, too, and even my wandering Uncle Nick. We celebrated until 3:00 a.m. when the new sheriff came and told us we were keeping the neighbors up, to all go home. We knew all the neighbors were right there, packed in Aunt Anna's back yard around the dancing sparks, but we went home anyway, quietly, docilely, the tiniest of embers from Anna's fire pit burning in each chest. It was a small victory.

The morning of the funeral was cool and clear with the first smell of impending fall. Later in the day it would be hot and windy. The dust would rise on the Sands and sweep through town as usual, but the angle of light through the swirling grit would carry that same, slight message of the morning, a change, a moving on.

Once again the door of the Church That Was Not Mormon and Was Not Catholic stood open. Miss Amelia was a devout Catholic, but Sal had strayed. Apprised of his renewed state of undress, and knowing of the close friendship between her brother and the Methodist-Minister-Without-a-Flock, she had opted for the rented church and the heartfelt, though often imponderable, words of the friend. Miss Amelia waited at the curb for the coffin, delivered by a tight-lipped, disapproving Udiah Simple.

You people! he hissed as the pallbearers slid the coffin from the hearse.

The six men, struggling under the twin weights of the coffin and appalling hangovers, were silent. Udiah Simple felt emboldened to add:

I wash my hands of the lot of you. Heaven will judge.

Miss Amelia answered for the men. She had come prepared. Stepping forward she lifted one of Simple's hands and placed Sal's oxfords in it.

I believe you wanted these, she said gently, then turned and followed the casket up the stairs and into the church.

The casket was placed on a low table beneath the pulpit at the front of the church. The top of the casket was opened, and Naked Sal's tanned nose was just visible above the oak side panels. Mourners arrived, all of Sixth Street, nursing headaches and a secret, followed by a handful of teenagers from above Main, nervous in foreign territory, who remembered Naked Sal's contributions to their education. The widows, in neat rows of black, their shoes two by two along the wood of the floor, filled the same rows they had for Gram's funeral. For a moment, I felt time ripple away from me, moving like a breeze across the surface of a clear pond, causing echoes on the water.

The Methodist-Minister-Without-a-Flock began to speak.

Friends, we are here to mourn Sal. He went around this community naked, but he was clothed in the friendship of many here today. He died alone, seemingly without that friendship. We must mourn that, too… .

Around the church, heads dropped under the weight of the words and then snapped upright as one of the heavy doors at the back of the church swung open. The minister blinked into a bright rectangle of light, and heads turned to watch a lean shape in a low-riding Fedora step into the church and close the door. Whatever the Methodist-Minister-Without-a-Flock had so eloquently begun was lost at the sight of the new sheriff. The sheriff stood at the back of the church, a narrow, dark exclamation mark to all the fear, shame, and sorrow the minister had perhaps hoped to assuage.

*Uh…uh…*his voice trembled. He looked over the pulpit and down at his silent friend in the coffin for inspiration and noticed for the first time Naked Sal's unobstructed tan.

Naked! the Methodist-Minister-Without-a-Flock squeaked.

The new sheriff's hat tipped back slowly as he looked down the aisle, across the brown nose of Naked Sal, and up at the minister. Heads swiveled and nervous glances circulated through the Sixth Street mourners. The widows, still unaware of the previous night's modest triumph and disproportionate celebration, crossed their arms over heavy bosoms and wondered at the hold-up. The Methodist-Minister-Without-a-Flock passed a shaking hand over his sweating forehead and coughed.

…Sal. Yes, Naked Sal, said the minister, his voice still high and strained. Recovering slightly, he added, *We come into this world naked… we leave this world naked. So shall Sal.*

The Methodist-Minister-Without-a-Flock cleared his throat again.

Perhaps we should pray, he suggested, his voice wobbling.

We dropped our heads and silently prayed. There was a creaking of wood and Aunt Anna rose, nudging Aunt Kiki to follow. Kiki grasped Mimi's hand. Trembling but obedient, the two followed Anna up the aisle to stand. They formed a dark-clad curtain in front of Naked Sal and paid their last respects. After a pause, all of Sixth Street joined them, the widows bringing up the rear. As people passed slowly by the casket they trailed down the side aisle of the church, along behind the back pews, and edged nervously around the new sheriff and out onto the steps of the church.

The first of the old women approached the coffin, black scarf pulled around her head and clutched under her chin.

Oh, mygolly!

In front of the open casket, Mrs. Pastervich was stopped dead in her tracks, hand paused in the midst of forming a cross. The widows accordioned in on her, bobbing and squabbling in a black clutch, trying to catch a peek at Sal. Theirs was the only movement and noise in the church. The retreating mourners had gone still and alert. The new sheriff leaned slightly to the left, seeking a view of the front of the church from around the people in his way. At the head of the gaggle of widows, pressed against Sal's coffin, Mrs. Pastervich leaned forward precariously and peered under the closed bottom section of the casket.

Mygolly, mygolly! she exploded again and popped upright in a movement that belied her years.

Black scarves and gray heads fluttered as the old women held an impromptu conference at the front of the church. Furious whispering, wild gestures, a cackle or two, and then a dozen wrinkled hands reached up together to close the coffin.

Amen! the Methodist-Minister-Without-a-Flock bellowed frantically.

Pallbearers! he cried.

The new sheriff turned on his heel and left the church.

157

At the graveside, the dust rose and swept across town and up the cemetery hill to sting our eyes and choke us. We sweated from relief and heat. As Miss Amelia silently cried, Sal was lowered into the grave. Someone tossed a quarter. We watched it cut through the thick, rushing air, its path a glinting arc in the wavering sun. It landed with a sharp ping on the brass fittings of the coffin. There was movement among the assembled crowd, a rifling of pockets and purses. The air was filled with a sudden, sparking shower of quarters. Two bits from thirty years of students. With each ping, Miss Amelia blinked and smiled.

On the ride home, Sofie asked, *Do you think somebody will dig Sal up for all those two-bit pieces? That's a lot of money.*

There was a long pause as we bumped over the gravel, and the worn shocks of Anna's car threw us around the back seat.

No one's gunna dig him up, said Paul disgustedly, rubbing his head where it had made contact with the window. *Except for maybe that new sheriff... .*

He wouldn't do that, would he? The new sheriff? Would he, Ma? Sofie asked.

Aunt Anna emitted a dark *Humph!* and jerked the car viciously onto the back top of the highway.

Who knows what that crazy chuvar will do, she said bitterly. *Here's a better question. Who will he pick on next, and what will we do? Who will stand up to him face to face and say NO?*

Sofie, Paul, and I exchanged a worried look and sank deeper into the back seat, seeking protection, protection from Anna's searching anger, protection from the notice of the new sheriff, protection from the vicissitudes of the road.

19

The unsaid drifted among dust motes in the slanting morning sun at Gram's kitchen table. *Don't go...* and *Why can't you just stay?* *...What's so special about college?* *...*and *Why do you have to go so far away?* I didn't want to say all that, it sounded too much like Aunt Anna. I didn't want to say, *I need you.* She would laugh and retort, *Don't you worry, Ma will take care of you.* I didn't want to say, *Who will cook for you, clean up after you? You need me.* That sounded like Aunt Anna, too. Josie's fur would rise. We both knew she could look after herself. So I didn't say anything. I watched her pore over the bus and train schedules, the wedge of hot pogacha bread unnoticed in front of her, its butter tracing a slow, yellow smear as it slid, melting, down the angle of the slice.

Eat your pogacha, I said.

She raised her head and grinned.

You sound just like Ma.

See, I muttered to myself.

What? she asked through a big bite of bread.

Nothing.

She waved her bread around and smacked the schedules with her other hand.

The problem is...the problem is how to get there. If I take the bus I can go from Parker, but I'll have to change buses four times and it will take forever. The train from Salt Lake is faster, and I only change in Chicago, but it costs a lot more and it means spending four hours in a car with Ma telling me why I shouldn't go.

You could throw your suitcases up on an ore car and travel like Uncle Nick... .

Josie stared at me, *Is that how he gets out of town? Huh. Leave it to you to know that. Well, thanks anyway, my father's means of locomotion are unappealing to me.*

It works for him, I retorted.

I want to arrive in Boston in style, not green from ore dust like a couple of girls of my acquaintance once were.

I smiled reluctantly across the table at her.

Hitchhike? I suggested.

Too dangerous.

Maybe someone around here's heading that way. I could ask around.

Josie shook her head and gave me her smile.

I want to arrive under my own steam.

She took a last bite of pogacha and brushed the crumbs from her hands and lap.

Mmmm, this is one thing I will miss, Gram's bread...your bread, now.

I'll send you loaves...or take me with you... .

She shook her head. *I don't need a thirteen-year-old mom. I have more than enough mom two doors down.* She grinned, *Nice try, though.*

I couldn't quite return the smile, so I busied myself gathering plates and cups.

I think Uncle Nick's finally home, I said, changing the subject.

Yah, I heard Ma yelling at 3:00 a.m., too. All of Sixth Street knows my dad's home. There'll be a long line for haircuts today.

Well, at least it's worth waiting for. Uncle Nick gives a clean cut, I said.

That's my dad, a true professional! Josie laughed.

I'm a little worried about him, Josie. I think I'll go up to the barbershop today to see him. I don't know how he's going to take Naked Sal's death. He might turn around and leave again.

Josie shrugged and gathered her purse and gloves from Eli's chair. Hesitating at the front door, she looked at me.

You know, you don't have to be everyone's keeper. Just be you.

This is me, I said quietly to the closing screen door. I went back to the kitchen.

This is what I do, I told the dirty breakfast dishes.

There's absolutely nothing wrong with caring about people, I grumbled to the blankets on Josie's bed as I brusquely straightened them.

I try to take care of people, I explained to the shirts and socks as I pulled them from the washing machine.

Even if some people don't appreciate it! I shouted at the wet laundry and gave the line a vicious push, sending two white blouses, a gray pleated skirt, and one dozen dripping panties sailing out to hang over the back yard.

Josie was Josie. I was who I was: Becky, Mala, youngest chartered member of the widow's club, mourner of old naked men and wandering uncles, friend to a whore's daughter, substitute mother to a college-bound woman. Me.

She is going to miss me so much, I promised the clear morning air and watched my words drift out from the back porch along the line of gently swaying laundry and out over the quiet, empty Sands.

I already knew I would tell her about Gram's car, the car that would make the trip to Boston so easy for her, get her there in style, under her own steam. I didn't want to, but I knew I would do it, tell her about the car that everyone had forgotten. Everyone but me, because that was who I was. That was my job. Listening… remembering…taking care…taking care of Josie. The car would be waiting for her when she came home from work. I picked up the phone and dialed Carrie.

It's me, I said to the sleepy hello. *Get a shovel and come down. I'll feed you breakfast.*

What time is it?

8:25.

Breakfast?

Yes.

And a shovel?

Yes.

Silence spun along the wire. I imagined her pushing her black curls from her face and scratching the back of her head. She liked to lounge in bed through most of the morning when she could. I suspected she acquired that from her mom's side of the family.

Okay, she yawned. *Twenty minutes.*

Gram had told me about the car. It was a 1936 Buick, paid for by Eli's wine money, money collected in six spare Ball jars and stored in his secret hiding place, a hole dug into the side of the cellar behind the open shelving bowed with dark, potent liquid. The empty hole was still there, four rows up, behind bottles eight and nine from the left. It was something everyone else had forgotten but me. The black Buick had spent only one year on the roads of Eastern Nevada, traveling once from Parker to Gram's home when it had been purchased. Once there, it made afternoon trips from the front of the house to the garage in back at the edge of The Sands in anticipation of the 2:00 p.m. dust storm, morning trips from garage to its place of honor in the front of the house and finally, Friday and Saturday night trips to the Taylor Club where it sat in the green glow of the street light until 1:00 a.m. when it lurched home and to rest. The car had never been driven out of first gear. Eli never acknowledged the need for shifting. He probably didn't know how. The inaugural trip from the car lot in Parker to Taylor had taken three hours and a tank of gas, the car whining at 5000 rpm and traveling a heady ten miles per hour. Gram cursed Eli at the top of her lungs three-quarters of the way, stopping only when she had run out of known vocabulary in Serb, English, Greek, and Italian. She completed the trip in stony silence, her arms crossed, her ears ringing with the car's high complaint.

All of Sixth Street had gathered to greet the proud new owners. They had been waiting an hour and a half. Eli pulled up in front of Gram's house and stopped the car. The radiator hissed with relief. Eli stepped out and stood next to his car amidst a throng of laughing, admiring neighbors. Gram refused to budge from the passenger seat, ticking in fury in time to the cooling car.

I tell you something, Eli addressed the crowd as he proudly patted the shiny black top of his first automobile. *She damn good car. Damn good. Maybe not so fast,* he shrugged philosophically. *But she strong. Lot of power. Roar like lion!*

The crowd cheered. An impromptu celebration began which lasted into the wee hours, and a nickname was instantly born. The Lion. *Here comes Eli in the Lion.* Gram used a different set of words to describe Eli and this the first, last, and only toy of his life: *Fool old man and nogoodgoddamnstupid car.*

After a year of being heard on the streets of lower Taylor, the Lion was permanently retired to the garage at the edge of The Sands behind the house. Eli had an accident at the mill. He was left with a left leg forever after stiff. Though he gained years of satisfaction from putting his stiff leg exactly where it would most be in the way of everyone else, he was never able to use it to ease the Lion from idle rest into the high adventure of first gear. Slowly, The Sands crept up around the garage, Eli died, and only Gram was left to tell the tale of Eli and the Lion.

Some day, Mala, Gram always ended the story, *Some day I give you Eli nogoodgoddamnstupid car. Maybe you drive right!*

Now the Lion was mine, to keep, to sell, to bestow.

We don't have to dig up the whole garage, I told Carrie as she wolfed down two slices of French toast thick with a sludge of butter and powdered sugar.

We just need to be able to get the door open and the car out.
Do you think she'll want a car that old?

Other than the brass up at the mill, Carrie's father was the only one in town who had a new car every two years. He said he needed a dependable car for all the house calls. He sold his used cars to the highest bidder. None of his used cars resided below Main. Maybe now that he, and by association his car, wore the taint of The Divine, the residents of Sixth Street might have a chance.

Oh, she'll want it. She might be pig-headed and annoying, but she's not dumb.

It probably doesn't even work anymore.

It can be fixed. Finish eating. We have a lot of digging to do.

It took us about two-and-a-half hours to uncover the front of the garage where it stood waist deep in shifted sand. The top layer was soft and easily moved aside, but each succeeding layer of sand and dirt was more compacted. The last layer, stone cold and hard, had to be picked at with the tips of our shovels. We were sweaty and filthy and very grouchy by the time we could pry the garage doors open and shove them, resisting and scraping, back to reveal the dark interior. The black car hunkered under an inch-thick layer of white dust sifted down through the corrugated tin roof. It looked ghostly and foreign, an ancient artifact uncovered from the sand of Egypt.

Josie's never going to appreciate all the effort it took to uncover that, Carrie said flatly.

She will once we wash it. Come on, let's push it out.

Carrie hesitated.

Things could have nested in there. Rattlesnakes.

I stopped in my tracks.

Or those little white scorpions, she added helpfully. *They're deadly.*

I gave her an evil look and dropped down on my hands and knees to check under the chassis. After gingerly edging my way around the car, I took a deep breath, yanked the driver's side door open, and jumped backwards. The car was still and empty. The keys, winking in a dusty ray of sunlight, swung from the ignition. I exhaled and breathed in an ancient, familiar smell.

I think the smell of Eli's cigars kept everything away.

Curious, Carrie joined me, draping an arm over my shoulder and leaning over to take a whiff.

Jeez, she reeled back. *Josie's not going to like that.*

We can leave it open while we wash it. That'll help...a little.

Well, we better wait. It's almost two.

So the Lion spent another Taylor dust storm in its den while Carrie and I listened to the radio and flipped through Josie's movie magazines. At 4:00 we unearthed the garage door yet again and pushed the car out into the afternoon sun. We borrowed two extra hoses from across the street, and fastening them together in a long, green, dripping snake, we washed the car and each other. Finally, the Buick sat gleaming like new, its wheels two inches deep in a slurry of sand, water, and dirt, its doors open to an elixir of evening air. We stood back to admire and then raced to the front yard to stand at the gate, dancing with anticipation, awaiting the first glimpse of Josie striding down Sixth Street. At first sight, we rushed to greet her and dragged her, laughing at us all the way, down the side of the house, across the back yard, under the dusty, forgotten laundry, and through the back gate to the half-buried garage and its disgorged contents, a sparkling 1936 Buick never driven out of first gear.

Oh my God! Oh my God!

It was the very first time I had known Josie to be near speechless.

It's for you, I told her.

It doesn't run, warned Carrie.

It will, I gave Carrie a shove.

Oh my God!

It was Eli's. Gram said I could have it someday.

Oh my God.

You can have it, Josie. You can go to college in it.

Josie walked over to the Buick as if a sudden move might startle it away. Muck oozed up over her red pumps. She didn't notice. She ran her long, brown fingers over the nose of the car and up its side toward the open driver's side door.

Oh my God, she whispered to herself.

It stinks, Carrie prepared her.

Josie, a hand on the top and a hand on the open door, leaned in and drew the car's essence in through her nose. She grinned at us over her shoulder.

I smell stale cigars…

She leaned back in, took another draught.

I smell old booze…maybe a hint of vomit…

She stuck her head back in once more, took a huge gulp of the interior, stood up, slammed the door and exhaled with a long *ahhh…* .

She threw her head back, and laughing, shouted, *I smell freedom!*

She rushed over to us and pulled us into the circle of her arms.

I am going to give you two the ride of your lives! she said, and squeezed us tightly.

It doesn't run, came Carrie's muffled voice.

I'll take care of that, Josie said, and leaned her head in close to ours. *Call all the cousins. Tell them to meet here after full dark. We'll push it to the end of Sixth Street and up the hill to Vinny Barbarini's garage on Main. Right past Ma's,* she added with relish.

With an arm around each of us, she led us through the gate and the back yard.

Under the caked, dusty line of laundry, she noted, *You forgot to bring in the clothes.*

Busy, I told her sheepishly.

She smiled, *That's a first. Did you get a chance to visit Dad?*

I shook my lowered head.

Well, well, well.

On the back steps she paused and asked, *Dinner?*

Busy, Carrie answered for me.

Another first, she drawled. *I guess I'll just have to treat you two to dinner at Mrs. Miniverri's In-Home Diner. We should be back just in time. I'll change my shoes.*

Later, she let me steer the heavy, resisting Buick down the dark street. She helped push. We eased past Aunt Anna's in a fit of muffled giggles.

It doesn't matter, Josie's voice clipped into the barely maintained quiet of the night and was rewarded with a loud chorus of *Shhh's.*

She might not have cared if Aunt Anna stepped outside and caught us, but every other niece and nephew who would continue to live with Aunt Anna's sharp, lingering justice certainly did. We were spared. Aunt Anna never materialized. Perhaps she was busy, cuffing and coddling by turns her recently returned husband. We glided on down the street, devising alibis for some future date when Aunt Anna was at last aware of our duplicity. The short hill up to Main proposed a minor problem, but with a running start and much strain and grunting we managed. I hopped out to steer and push together. When the car sat glinting in the light of the street lamps before Vinny Barbarini's garage door, we stopped, gave a furtive cheer, and slapped each other's backs before parting ways and slipping off in twos and threes to home.

Back at Gram's house, in the deep hollow of Gram's couch, Josie and I listened to the radio low. Pressed together, we were connected at hip and shoulder, but separated more than ever by the future. She read the *Parker Press Times*, folded neatly down to a single article. I stared at my book, the black lines blurred and meaningless.

Do you remember at the beginning of the summer? she

asked, never raising her head. *When you dressed in Gram's apron and slippers and wore your hair like her? You've come a long way.*

I nodded and blinked, dropping my head a little, trying to make sense of Huck Finn.

You're like her in other ways, though, she told me softly. *Generous with everything, looking out, giving.*

The music was no more than a murmur, wrapping us in its quiet, light veil, making her words like secrets.

I'm not like that, she told me.

It was part confession, part warning. I did not want to say anything, to acknowledge or dispel. We sat touching, tied together by the thin gauze of low music.

It's not a bad thing, she sighed out, her lips hardly moving.

And I did not know to which of us she referred.

20

Eating at Mrs. Miniverri's In-Home Diner was an experience both sublime and strange. The food could not have been more heavenly if a host of angels had delivered it, still steaming sweetly, from celestial kitchens. But there were rules. No matter what the time of year, you left your shoes outside, in the summer on the grass, in the winter on the wide, covered, double-carpeted porch. Laundered daily, knitted red wool slippers with large white dingleballs waited like British soldiers in neat lines along the sides of the front door. Once in slippers and through the door, you walked to your table slowly. You didn't speak. Not one word, a cough, nor a sneeze. The bottoms of the chair legs and the tops of tables were heavily padded in felt, and you were expected to sit, eat, pay, and slip away in total quiet. You chewed quietly; you never slurped your soup; your fork never scraped your plate. A burp would have been the highest treason, requiring a long, hungry exile. However, Mrs. Miniverri's dinners seldom required such human responses as a belch, a slurp, an ugly struggle with a bit of gristle. Mrs. Miniverri's soups were velvet, her meats and vegetables so tender they fell apart beneath a sharp glance, her breads and deserts so light they almost floated to your lips. But not even a sigh of blissful satisfaction was allowed. The rule was silence. The reason was Johnny Miniverri.

Johnny Miniverri was troubled by air currents. They spoke to him. They whispered their secrets. They told him things he didn't want to know. A slight sound, a quick, thoughtless movement stirred the restless air, sent it seeking Johnny, complaining, arguing, worrying him as if he were a bone being gnawed by rats. He had to listen to the air currents. They were everywhere. He could go into his special closet with its layers of thick quilts nailed to the walls and door. He could take his special blue blanket (blue is a quiet color) and stuff it into the crack beneath the door. He could sit still in the dark, but they were out there, the air currents, testing the hinges, fingering the blanket that bulged thick and soft from beneath the door, seeking, waiting with the inevitability of breath for the one who had to listen.

Sometimes, in moments of courage, he talked back. He argued.

I'm not listening to you! at the blank ceiling.

Don't you say that!

Don't!

Don't!

He'd scream so the whole town could hear. He'd smash his palms against his ears. At those times, his mother would come to him, smelling of bread and spices, of onions browned in olive oil. She would take his hands from his ears and hold them in one of hers while she stroked his hair and rubbed his knotted back. Everywhere she touched became a strong spot and still. She spoke so quietly it was almost a thought. She'd try to get him to eat something. He'd try too, for her, but winced with every motion of his jaw as he chewed. He swallowed, so slowly, so carefully.

There were times when he could almost become a rock, a cliff face, a mountain, immovable to fretful air or sound. But those times were not often, and the last one was long ago. Mostly, he hid.

Eating at Mrs. Miniverri's In-Home Diner, you never saw Johnny, but he was there, in his room, in his closet. He was part of the atmosphere, the hushed expectancy of each sublime bite. You could feel his listening in the still air. From the dark, padded closet, he measured your mouthfuls, waiting for the moment when molar scraped against molar. He braced himself for the careless exhalation of enjoyment, the sigh that would stir the unseen and send him spiraling. Still, the diners came, to help Mrs. Miniverri keep her crazy son, and to taste the excess of love that resided in each dish.

We had Shepherd's Pie the night we let Eli's car out of its cave and opened its four doors to the breeze and washed it till it shined. Shepherd's Pie. Thick chunks of lamb with carrots and onions crowded in a gravy heavy with wine and rosemary, all hiding beneath a crisped layer of mashed potatoes. There was roasted garlic soup and brown bread, too, a salad in a lemony dressing and a custard pie that tasted of cream and burnt sugar and cinnamon. We were part of the five-o'clock seating, one of the two tables in the back bedroom, Mrs. Miniverri's bedroom. The other eight tables were scattered through the kitchen and the front room. All were full. The front bedroom was Johnny's, empty of tables of course, its thin door closed, locked, silently throbbing like a wound.

When we left at a quarter to seven, Mrs. Miniverri hugged us each at the door, kissed us noiselessly, refused to accept Josie's money. She loved to feed young people. Outside on the porch steps the seven-o'clock diners sat, slipping out of their pumps and loafers, pulling on their bright slippers, adjusting their dingleballs. Seven o'clock was mostly an uptown crowd, somber local businessmen and mine managers with their primped wives. They could sit, eat, pity, disapprove, and leave thoroughly satisfied in body and spirit. We flounced our way through them, matching their disdain with our own less refined brand. We took our shoes to the street to put them on.

Josie was still holding the six one-dollar bills in her hand. She shook her head and stuffed the money into her purse, the angry snapping of the catch echoing in the empty street. I knew her. She didn't like the responsibility that came with not paying. She raked long fingers through her hair, shook her heavy mane from her neck, and set off at a brisk pace up the hill towards Carrie's street to drop her off. We ran to keep up.

It's crazy to run a business and not charge, Josie muttered.

She just likes to see us eat, Josie. Because he won't.

Mala's right. That just shows how crazy he is. He won't eat her cooking!

Josie threw up her hands, *He's crazy. She's crazy. This whole town's crazy!*

Well, Josie, at least Johnny can't help it, I said.

Yah, agreed Carrie. *He sure can't help it. Gosh, remember last year? He was outside talking to the rafters on the porch or something, and a big old mill truck rattled by? Oh, boy! That was amazing,* Carrie told us with relish. *He went through the streets like a banshee. Sheriff Billy followed him way out onto The Sands. A lot of people did. My dad had to go out there and give him a shot while Sheriff Billy held him. A sedative. Then they carried him back and put him in his closet. It was like a parade through the middle of town. I don't think he's been outside since.*

That's my point exactly, Josie countered. *A parade! Johnny Miniverri might be the only one who's certifiable, but the rest of the town's not far behind. What about poor Naked Sal? What about that new sheriff? He's even kookier than Sheriff Billy was. What about my own dad? People in this town can't even get a haircut because he's wandered off somewhere.* Josie shook her head. *And they don't even mind! Trust me, this whole town is nuts.*

I could have added to her list. There was Uncle Milan, who made his secret shoes and slipped them into old ladies' houses in the dead of night. There was Carrie's father, who could cure others but not himself. There was my own mother, maybe. And there was a clutch of old ladies dressed in black, who prayed and watched and turned the Wheel of fate. Maybe Josie was right. We had to be crazy to stay in a town where nature spit dust in our faces every afternoon, where a Copper King ruled our lives. But there was more to Taylor than that. I thought of Sixth Street's wild parties, the family gatherings, the old stories retold with endless enjoyment, the neighbors' willing, helping hands. I thought of Carrie's father and the whore named The Divine, of Mrs. Miniverri, her food and her son. There was something here that didn't need a reason. Love.

172

Commitment.

I wanted to marry him, I suddenly told them.

They stopped and stared at me.

Johnny Miniverri. I wanted to marry him. He used to baby-sit me sometimes.

Here, I gave Josie a quick, accusing glance. She had never wanted to. Baby-sitting for family meant no pay.

It was before, when he was okay. Sometimes Gram used to go off to Parker with the Methodist-Minister-Without-a-Flock to gamble her pension check. Gram would drop me off at Mrs. Miniverri's and Johnny would watch me. A quarter an hour. I bit him once. I must have been about five-years-old. He wanted me to go inside and I didn't want to. So I bit him. He tasted sweet, like his mom's honey buns. He didn't get mad. He just laughed. He was so beautiful, and he tasted good, too. I decided right then and there I was going to marry him. I told him so. He said okay. He was nine years older than me. I told him he had to stop at twenty and wait for me. He said he'd do that. It lasted until he came back from the V.A. hospital after boot camp.

He's twenty-two, now, Josie said.

Yah, I know, I said. *He was so different when he came back, I figured he wouldn't want to anymore.*

Josie looked at me and asked softly, *What about you?*

Well, he's still beautiful...and I bet he still tastes of his mom's honey buns....

Josie laughed then, a clear, ringing sound of delight. She put her arm around my shoulder.

You are just as crazy as the rest of them.

I smiled up at her.

Yep.

At the gate of Carrie's house we stood and said our good-byes. In the kitchen, Carrie's father sat in a pool of light at the table, patiently waiting. For Carrie, for The Divine.

We were not a town of crazy people. We were a town of

people waiting, waiting for haircuts, for jobs, for acceptance, for the dust to settle. A Methodist Minister waited for a flock. Mrs. Miniverri and I waited for her son to return to us. Johnny waited for deliverance. A group of widows waited for the Holy Wheel to turn. Even Josie waited. She waited for the moment when Eli's car was fixed and she drove it, roaring, out of this town. Then all her waiting would be over.

21

Everyone on Sixth Street knew the Miniverri's story, but my favorite telling was by the widow's club, their woven voices urging small details on me like offerings of tasty morsels, their hands shaping the words in the guarded space of our circle. Mrs. Miniverri was a member of the widow's club, though she was not a widow and she never had time to gather with the other members to gossip or swap ailments. Still, the other women felt she had gone through so much that she had earned her right to membership, despite the fact of the husband.

What kind of husband that? Mrs. Andervitic snorted with scorn. *He never home. Never! Never help.*

What man ever help? another gray head cawed.

There was a flurry of flapping sweaters and cackling laughter.

Old Joe help just once Johnny. Remember?

The group quieted. They nodded their heads sadly and began their story.

Joe Miniverri was a Basque sheepherder, brought over from the Old Country long ago with many of his countrymen to herd in the vast emptiness of the high western plains. He lived in a shepherd's wagon with a couple of dogs and followed his flock as it chased summer into high mountain valleys where the grass was lush and green from glacial runoff and the air was so thin that to breathe it felt like swallowing a knife. In early fall they wandered together down onto endless sagebrush flats where towering dust devils could carry off a handful of sheep in a whirling moment and send them dancing though the sky like surprised wallflowers pressed into sudden service at a dance. He lived months at a time without ever seeing another human being. The emptiness and silence of the endless landscape seeped into him, and he became light with it. His footsteps swept away in the wind, the tracks of his wagon lost in dense turf or on hard rock. He thought to himself, here is a land no man could mark. He loved it. It took him nine years to decide to fulfill his promise and bring his patient bride-to-be from the Old Country.

In the Basque Mountains just over the French border, the eventually-to-be Mrs. Miniverri had spent the nine years hard at work. Slowly she built up money for her boat fare and then waited. Her brothers built her a dowry chest. As the years passed and she waited, they carved it with the vines of a climbing rose, added buds and flowers, a sprinkle of petals beneath and birds light as air above. Mrs. Miniverri took over the family cooking and rewarded the brothers with a discovered artistry of her own. As the chest grew in beauty, she filled it with linens of her own making and other items given or dearly bought. And always, she waited.

She have two candlesticks from her mamma and poppa. Silver!

Pots, pans, forks, knives, too—good things people give her.

Gray heads nodded eagerly; they loved tolling treasures and tragedies.

And she learn English, too, Mala. From book from Priest.

She already speak Spanish and French.

And Basque.

Sure she speak her own language, old fool!

Humph!

Language come easy her, this said soothingly, to smooth ruffled feathers and ease the story forward.

She have long time to learn. Wait long time for Old Joe.

Too long. Stay home, no trouble then.

There was a general nod of agreement, until one voice pointed out,

Go, stay, no difference. Trouble always find.

This, too, was true, requiring another nod, a sign of the cross and a gentle turn of the Holy Wheel.

Whatever Mrs. Miniverri should have done, go is what she

176

did. She and her dowry chest took a boat headed to New Orleans from the port of Marseilles. A late-season hurricane pulled the ship off course and broke it apart on the far western Gulf. Mrs. Miniverri saw her dowry chest float past as the ship's lifeboats struck out for the Mexican coast. For three days, Mrs. Miniverri refused to budge from the beach, hoping the chest would wash ashore.

Nothing, Mrs. Colodopolous shook her head sadly. *No chest, no pots, no candlestick, nothing!*

Those candlesticks silver, too!

The circle took a moment to turn the Holy Wheel and say a silent prayer for the sunken riches.

Well? I asked, though I knew the story so well I could have told it to them.

She go north, Mrs. Pintar said and pointed up.

Mrs. Miniverri made her way on foot from Tampico to Metamores and then to the U.S. border. Joined by fifty other secret, night crossers, Mrs. Miniverri crawled through cactus for two miles. She heard the laughter of bored guards as they took potshots at the darkness. She heard the tufts of sound as bullets pocked the sandy earth around her.

I tell you they probably kill her, they find her!

A shudder ran through the circle of old women. They were experiencing their own run-in with authority, and this part of the story held new resonance.

In Brownsville, Texas, Mrs. Miniverri worked as a cook in a hotel and slept on a cot in the kitchen until she had enough money for the train to Nevada. The hotel manager begged her to stay.

She big business. Everybody come, eat.

She know then, she pretty damn good cook.

Best cook whole world. Mrs. Pintar spread her heavy arms to emphasize the extent of Mrs. Miniverri's art.

Make best soup.

Pie, bread, too!

And meat...oh, mygolly!
Lots of garlic.

Yes, they all agreed. Maybe that was the secret. This was high praise from these women who eyed each other's offerings and secret ingredients with scorn. Mrs. Miniverri was regarded in a class of her own. She always shared her recipes freely, took time to explain her methods: a pinch of this, a handful of that, never put the oven on too high a flame, rub the spices into the meat with warm hands and lots of olive oil. But the reproductions never measured up to the original. There was always some indefinable element missing.

Best cook whole goddamn world, right here Taylor.

They nodded proudly. They were happy to give her this distinction; she was their comrade, their sister. She had so little else.

After Mrs. Miniverri arrived in Taylor, she lived in the basement of the Catholic Church. She cooked and cleaned for the priest while Joseph Miniverri was sought and found and brought back from some distant corner of western plains. The priest, after the first week of Mrs. Miniverri's residence, began hinting to God in his nightly prayers that perhaps it would be just fine if Joe was not found, that Joe might be happier alone with his sheep, that Mrs. Miniverri (who really wasn't Mrs. Miniverri yet, the priest pointed out) should remain in the basement and cook. God didn't listen. Joe showed up three weeks later, dusty, nervous, and silent. Mrs. Miniverri wasn't silent. She had a lot to tell Joe, ten years now of news and adventures. All through the hasty service, she apologized continually for losing her dowry. Joe never said a word more than *I do.* He was overwhelmed by the noise of her. He tried to breathe in the narrow silences between her sentences. By dawn the next morning, Joe was up, packed, and ready to return to his sheep. Mrs. Miniverri wasn't invited. From her bed, she watched him climb the basement stairs of the church. She didn't mind his going. She had found out in the last eighteen hours that he wasn't much company. He didn't have much to say for himself. She tried to remember him from before. She shrugged and crossed her arms across her chest. She was not one to give up. Later that morning, she went to talk to the priest.

She say that priest, I cook you pay. Priest say yes. She give him breakfast.

She no want live in no basement. She save money, buy own house. Not company house, own house! Back then, only one from Old Country with own house.

She see how people keep saying priest, maybe I come over have little dinner with you. She think, Maybe I make little more money.

She buy tables, feed people in own house. Pretty soon, making big money. Saving.

All the time wait for Joe, though.

Take whole year come back, that one!

Humph! A grumble of annoyance circulated through the room. The stupidity of men was legendary in this circle.

However, not one of them could deny that when Joe finally returned, he did make an effort. He told her about his sheep, his dogs, the coyotes and mountain lions that were a constant threat. Mrs. Miniverri had a lot to tell Joe, but she tried not to. She listened to him, counted his sentences, about twenty in all. She was encouraged. She decided to close the In-Home Diner for the length of his stay. He played his harmonica on the front porch. She cooked him a meal. He was unwilling to be coaxed into their new home, so she served him dinner on the porch steps, and together they listened to the crickets. It was hard, but he came in to sleep. The next morning, he was ready to leave again. Mrs. Miniverri had breakfast waiting, honey buns hot from the oven and eggs baked in cream with a sprinkle of paprika, ham fried with onions and red pepper and a hint of garlic.

I'll be back, he said as he stood from the table.

Okay, Joe, she told him. *I'll be here.*

By noon, Mrs. Miniverri's In-Home Diner was open for business. And that's how it went, with Joe returning maybe once or twice a year, stepping through the door like a man walking into a minefield, hardly saying a thing while he stayed and leaving a day later, well-fed but relieved at his release. Distance being the surest form of birth control, it was eight years before Joe's sporadic returns brought him the surprise of a three-month-old baby boy in a crib by the oven.

So beautiful baby!

Everyone nodded enthusiastically.

Like something she make in kitchen, perfect!

We were quiet for a time. I remembered skin that tasted of honey and cinnamon and laughing blue eyes. Perhaps they thought of how precariously perfection stood at the top of their Holy Wheel, where there is only one direction to go.

Johnny beautiful baby...and good, too.

They agreed sadly.

Joe held the baby gently, like the newborn sheep he sometimes needed to help into the world. It made little animal noises and smelled of lanolin and wildflowers. Between the baby and the food, Joe was inclined to think his wife a miracle worker. He stayed three days that time. It was the closeness that drove him off, the breath and warmth and motion of another body next to him in bed, the noises held in by walls and ceilings or exaggerated in the narrow alley that ran behind the house. In his world all noise was offered up and lost in the limitless quiet of the sky. Out there, he could lay on the ground with his head on a rock and feel everything in him rise, drifting upward with the heat and the sounds of the earth released at dusk, leaving him still, empty, clean.

I'll be back, he said to Mrs. Miniverri as she stood on the front porch with Johnny on her hip.

Okay, Joe. I'll be here. She watched him go and then returned to her kitchen.

Johnny grew up like his mother, loving to talk and laugh,

multi-lingual, and good in school. He was a charmer, a heart-throb, eclipsed only by the returning G.I.s, swaggering and worldly in their pressed uniforms. He watched them with envy. He wanted that uniform. He had missed the war, but that didn't stop him. On his eighteenth birthday, he enlisted and six weeks later was in boot camp in North Carolina. It was in boot camp that Johnny broke into pieces and even the uniform couldn't hold him together. Some essential part of him never came home.

They mean him that camp! Mrs. Colodopolous erupted accusingly.

They no good. They make him crazy, Mrs. Pintar nodded in agreement.

No, no, Mrs. Andervitic corrected knowingly. *In Old Country, Mrs. Miniverri have crazy uncle. Same thing.*

He just like Old Joe, I think, only maybe little bit more… .

I say camp do it!

I tell you uncle, same thing Johnny!

They could not agree or compromise; they shook their heads at each other and stubbornly crossed their arm over their breasts, each old woman a thick, weighty block of opinion, unwilling to budge. Finally, Mrs. Casteverri waved them all off, cuffing the air of the circle with a hand crabbed with arthritis.

Johnny have 'frenia'. Mrs. Miniverri tell me so. She say 'frenia.'

They were silent for a minute, regrouping in the face of first-hand testimony and medical terminology.

I say, Mrs. Colodopolous said at last with a deep, wise nod of her head. *I say, what the hell that thing 'frenia'? what the hell that? Who give Johnny that? Boot camp!*

Schizophrenia, probably brought on by the mental and physical stress. The VA Hospital treated him with ice baths and shock treatments. There was no medicine. Once he was no longer in a straight jacket or curled in a fetal position in the corner of the ward, he was discharged from the army and placed in his mother's custody. On the long drive home, Johnny winced as he watched the words come from his mother's mouth. He put his hands over his ears and crouched against the passenger door. She saw she would not be able to cajole him back to health. The rest of the long car trip from the East Coast was completed in silence.

He spent whole days arguing with invisible assailants.

Go away! Go away, he'd beg. *Please, please be quiet.*

He plugged his ears and watched his mother's feet as they tapped purposefully in their black widow shoes around the tables set for diners, as she moved from sink to stove. When customers came, he plastered himself into the corner of his closet, braced himself for the clink of dishes, the dangerous rattle of cutlery and the air currents they caused, invisible shock waves set off and searching, for him. When the mill whistle blew from atop its towering smokestack every day at eight and noon, three and eleven, Mrs. Miniverri joined him in the closet and held him tight, keeping him from banging the echo from his head. When the wind rose in the afternoon and the dust tapped like fingernails against the window and the eaves of the porch moaned, Johnny cried. Worst of all, he wouldn't eat.

I can hear my food being digested, he whispered, and turned his head away from the plate.

What Mrs. Miniverri came to understand was that Johnny's need for silence, his need for stillness was so elemental it was like water or air for anyone else. It was what nourished him. She sent for Joe.

That most terrible thing of all, Mala, Mrs. Pintar whispered to me, and all around me heads nodded sadly.

Ol Joe, he take Johnny up to mountains. He think nice and quiet up there with his sheep. He think Johnny like better. He try be good papa.

There was general grumbled disagreement. For these

182

women, the only place for a sick child was with its mother.

Ol Joe try to be good papa, Mrs. Pintar insisted. *No his fault!*

There were different kinds of silence, but Joe did not know that then. The restful emptiness of the landscape with its quiet noises that signified the absences of so much more brought peace and joy to Joe. To Johnny, it was a long, unbuffered scream. The wind tossing the trees and sage, fingering the dry grass, the sheep with their mutterings and restless movement, the scratching of the dogs, the startling howl of coyotes, the crackling of the fire, the tick of the earth as it cooled at night, sounds stirred the voices that whispered insistently to him. He was in the wide open, easy for the voices to find. He walked beside his father like a man both shell-shocked and braced for the next bomb to fall. And then, the bomb fell.

They test atom bomb. Ol Joe and Johnny in mountains right above that valley. See whole thing.

The group of women shook their heads disgustedly. They could not believe the government could do such a thing with poor Johnny Miniverri right there to see, to hear it all. They would have given the government an earful if it had been there in the room at that moment.

Take Joe three days find Johnny. Johnny very sick, no water, no food. So crazy now, no move, no nothing.

Joe take Johnny home. Johnny go hospital, sick long time.

Hospital no want give Johnny back.

Poor mama, nothing do but wait.

And cook.

They nodded solemnly.

This time when Johnny came home, Mrs. Miniverri would be ready for him. The floor was carpeted wall to wall, the tables heavily padded in felt. No chair would scrape, no cutlery clatter. She amended herself as well. She nodded to her customers, pointed them to their seats, smiled her acknowledgement at compliments and thanks. She practiced silence.

We make slipper for Mrs. Miniverri. Red with white ball. Many, many.

They nodded proudly.

Colors my idea, Mrs. Andervitic told me.

Oh, you, someone muttered.

Mrs. Miniverri, she tell people, you wear slipper, you eat. So everybody wear slipper.

They cackled appreciatively. The image of those uptown people in their Sixth Street slippers was a constant source of mirth and delight.

Mrs. Miniverri joined her guests in their new fashion statement, but she wore her red slippers with the oversized, white dingleballs all the time. Her standard-issue, black widow shoes, courtesy of the unknown Taylor shoe fairy, were banished to the front porch, where they were used only for trips to the market for supplies. She padded Johnny's closet with layer after of layer of quilts, tested the sounds that seeped through and padded some more. At last she was ready. She collected her son.

It took another year before the father, Joe, came home again. The silence he found there was profound, frightening. Not open and undulating like in his beloved mountains and plains, here the silence was claustrophobic, thick as bitter smoke. He coaxed his wife onto the porch, pointed and whispered about the stars. He held her hand, and she, who had always been the stronger one, held his back. He tried to stay three days, managed only two. On the morning he left he went to the dry goods store. He came back with the blue blanket and handed it to her on the porch.

For under Johnny's door, he said.

She nodded.

I'll be back, he told her.

Okay, Joe, she said. *We'll be here.* Cradling the blue blanket in her arms, she watched him walk out the yard.

It was as if we had conjured him with our story that day in late August, as if our voice had reached him in the still space of his vacuum, and discerning it from all the other whispering voices that haunted him, he had listened and come out. He was on the porch when the noon whistle blew. Mrs. Miniverri, powdered up to her elbows in cake flour, came through the front of the house like a shot and lunged for him, but her slippers caught on the thick carpeting of the porch and her grip was made ineffective by the flour. Johnny slipped by her and bolted toward the street, powdery fingerprints still clutching his arms. He ran down Main, swatting at the air around his head as if a hundred yellowjackets pursued him. The quiet of midday Taylor was sliced open by his thin, high scream. The new sheriff came to the door of his office to watch Johnny pass. He went back inside to collect his hat, came out, climbed into his car, and followed. From behind the plate glass windows of shops, people watched first Johnny and then the sheriff's blue Buick head for the edge of town.

Outside of town, Johnny, still swatting but now too winded to scream, followed Highway 50 to the point where it met the rough dirt road that ran at right angles to the highway, up to the cemetery, or down to the Taylor pool. Without hesitation he ran toward the pool. The new sheriff had caught up to Johnny by now. He didn't try to stop him. From six feet behind, the blue Buick nosed down the deeply rutted road, following Johnny's stumbling, chaotic progress. Twice he tripped, fell, rolled. The Buick slowed, like a tracking beast, then eased forward once Johnny, now bleeding and dusty, was again on his feet and moving.

The Taylor pool was a deep, sandy hole in the ground, ringed by ancient cottonwoods and fed by a cold spring that ran underground from the mountains. About sixty kids were there the noon that Johnny visited. A few moms from uptown sat in the shade and kept an eye on their pink and white children. Carrie was there, in her cherry red bathing suit that set

185

the women in the shade on edge and made them nudge each other and whisper about the sins of the fathers and how fruit didn't fall far from the tree.

Johnny came barreling down the hill and across the sandy beach, trailed closely by the sheriff in his blue Buick. All gossip and play ceased as moms and kids stilled to watch Johnny Miniverri, swatting at thin air and fully clothed run into the water and disappear. Seconds spun out as the Buick slowly braked and the sheriff stepped out. He stood at the edge of the water and surveyed the flat, still surface of the pond. Carrie told me later that she thought the new sheriff would just turn around and leave, but he didn't. In his worn-at-the-heel boots and felt fedora he waded into the clear, cold water. At about waist-deep he bent over and pulled Johnny up by his collar. He dragged him ashore, slapped him into the back of his Buick, and left. The kids on the hot sand of the beach and standing, goose-pimpled in the icy water of the pool watched Johnny, his hand pressed to his ears, ride up the hill toward the highway until the blue Buick was lost in its own dust. Then they started to play again. The moms underneath the tree raised their eyebrows at each other and, leaving the subject of Carrie behind, moved on to this other issue.

The new sheriff brought Johnny back to Mrs. Miniverri's house and handed him over, wet and shivering, to his agitated mother. Mrs. Miniverri had had two run-ins with the new sheriff already, one about a business license and one when the new sheriff had finally heard about Johnny and had come to check things out. Mrs. Miniverri had heard what was said of the new sheriff, too, on her trips to the market and post office. She had expected no less than that the new sheriff would shoot her Johnny. When he simply turned from the front door and left, the relief that washed over Mrs. Miniverri was so intense that she had to sit at one of the tables for a few minutes. Tears ran down her face and fell noiselessly on the table top, creating a cryptogram of spots and blotches on the thick, green felt. In the kitchen, the egg timer when off. Johnny jumped and rushed to his bedroom and the closet. From the front room, she heard the closet door click carefully closed. Mrs. Miniverri rose and went to rescue her cake. Twenty minutes later, the new sheriff was back, knocking at the front door with a noise that ran through the house like rifle shots. He spoke without preamble.

I'll have that boy put away if I see him on my streets again, he told Mrs. Miniverri. He handed her a Johnson's heavy-duty padlock, strapped down to its square of yellow cardboard, showing a green and white price sticker from the dry goods store.

She weighed the padlock in her hand and thought it heavier that any iron pot full of soup that she had carried, any carcass of lamb she had hoisted to the kitchen counter to be butchered and trimmed.

I have some nice cake, Sheriff. Just warm from the oven. Would you like a slice to take? she asked and raised her eyes from the padlock, but the new sheriff was already gone.

Still carrying the lock, she went into Johnny's bedroom to check on him. She gently opened the door and looked inside. Wrapped in his blue blanket, Johnny crouched in the back. In the dark space of the closet, she could see the whites of Johnny's eyes beneath the deep black of his wet hair. His hands were still pressed to his ears.

Someone is screaming, he told her. *Who is it?*

22

Vinnie Barbarini's garage was at the very end of Main in what had once been a two-room house. Vinnie had widened the front door to accommodate an automobile. The front room became the garage. It still sported patches of smeared, sooty wallpaper with delicate yellow roses and a grease-blackened carpet that showed signs in the corners of once having been blue. The second room, the kitchen, acted as Vinnie's home. There was a stove, a sink, a table, a chair, and a bed. All this had been reported by Stanley Kurkopec who had had occasion to carry Vinnie home from the Taylor Club on Sunday nights. Few people had ventured beyond a few feet within the double door of the garage. They were deterred by the filth. There was a third room—actually, a bathroom—connecting the front room to the kitchen. No one had ever been in there. From the state of Vinnie and his many peculiar habits, it had been concluded that he, in fact, had never used this room, except perhaps as a conduit from his work to his stove and his bed. The bathroom didn't count.

Vinnie Barbarini was a terrific mechanic. No one knew how old he was or when he had arrived from the Old Country. No one remembered the previous owners of the two-room house, the lovers of yellow roses and sky blue carpet. Vinnie's Garage and he had sat at the end of Main for as long as anyone could remember. No one had seen him out of his mechanic's coverall. It was surmised he slept in it. Its original color had been lost. The widows thought Vinnie had grown from some sort of mold in that bathroom.

He never clean that room, Mrs. Markovich would say, shaking her finger at her circle of grinning friends. *I tell you. He grow there!* Her eyes would twinkle.

Ei me! They'd groan delightedly, shake their heads, and reach for handkerchiefs that waited, secured between ample bosoms.

Never clean toilet. That one never clean own body!

No, no. Vinnie no want to melt!

The room would ring with cackling laughter and faces would be swabbed of tears.

No need clean, be good mechanic, someone would always say finally, and the circle would smile, tear-moist, and nod in agreement.

Vinnie started out working only on Fords. There was no use asking. Cadillacs, Chryslers, Buicks all had to be driven or towed to Parker or beyond for work. Then, in the early thirties, a Hollywood starlet attempted to race through Taylor between two and four one Saturday afternoon in mid-August. Her car, a red convertible Cadillac already burdened with two thousand miles of open road, gasped its last in front of the Taylor Club. She was stuck. Thank you, Taylor Daily Dust Storm. Like the color of Vinnie's coverall, the identity of the starlet has been lost, some say Hedy Lamar, some say Garbo or Dietrich. Every five years or so, the debate rears its platinum head and there are fistfights in the Taylor Club. She came with a manager of some sort, wrapped in a pale suit and dark glasses and with a nervous personal secretary-type woman. The entire contents of the Taylor Club rolled out of the swinging doors to push the red Cadillac into Vinnie's Garage. The red car came to rest on the blackened front room carpet. The crowd waited for his pronouncement, grinning, knowing what would happen, what he would say. Vinnie rubbed his hair into stiff spikes, wiped his hands on his coverall, pulled on his left ear, chewed his mangled pencil, then stuck it up his nose, pulled it out, examined it, smoothed his eyebrows, did a quick two-step, scratched his chest, did another quick two-step, scratched his head, put his pencil in his mouth, surveyed the ceiling for cracks…. Outside the dust storm proceeded.

I work on Fords.

The little group of foreigners was offered the accommodations of some empty miners' quarters above the bar. The man in pale suit and sunglasses spent the rest of the afternoon and evening on the Taylor Club's phone talking to California. The nervous secretary wept. The starlet drank a whole bottle of Jack Daniels, neat. Her glass is enshrined behind the bar, its kiss of bright red lipstick unfaded after all these years. Around two a.m., the starlet stood from her stool at the bar and walked to the swinging doors of the Taylor Club. She paused and smiled at the packed house and then disappeared into the darkness outside. The even click of her heels echoed down the sidewalk toward Vinnie's. Every imagination in Taylor followed her that night, through the cool air along the street, into the blackness of the open garage, through the dark, jungle mystery of that bathroom and into the kitchen with its stove and sink, its table, chair, and bed. Vinnie in his coverall sitting on his chair probably proved a stumbling block to those imaginations, as no doubt, it must have been to the starlet herself. But then, anything really worthwhile takes a little effort.

In the morning, again perched at the Taylor Club's bar, the starlet ate bacon and eggs, washed down with more whiskey brought to her by the red-eyed secretary. The manager was on the phone. Sounds of industry emitted from Vinnie's garage. Before she settled into the back seat of her Cadillac a few minutes before 9:00 a.m., the starlet ran her red fingernails along Vinnie's cheek and smiled her thanks. Transfixed, he stopped his odd dancing, his scratching and picking, and offered her the smeared receipt. The Cadillac was already gone. Vinnie watched the dust trail drift and settle in the street. He looked down at the white receipt, still extended from his fingers. He rubbed his eyebrows, he scratched his chest, he stuck his finger in his ear and performed a delicate, swaying pirouette, all the while staring at the receipt. He smiled, shoved the slip of paper in his mouth and began to chew.

After that, he worked on anything, a Lincoln, a Mercury, even an occasional International Harvester tractor....

When Josie walked through the door that afternoon we could tell this was it. Sitting in a circle on Gram's front room floor, scattered coins and playing cards around us, we ceased our nervous figuring and stared at her.

The car, she said. *Is ready.*

She picked her way between us and stood for a moment in the middle of our circle, over the pot of pennies and nickels.

I'm after cash. She smiled down at me, *Becky, you come with me.*

Black Jack! Sofie hollered, slammed down an ace of diamonds and ten of spades, and scooped the pot from between Josie's pumps. Our attention shifted. We groaned and tossed our useless cards up in the air.

Josie laughed, the cards cascading around her skirt and littering the toes of her pumps.

I'll take you all to Parker for burgers and shakes after I register the car at the courthouse.

Eli's Buick, now Josie's, had required a new battery and four new tires. Entombed in the cool, dry air of the buried garage behind Gram's house, it had survived the years well. Vinnie Barbarini had thrown in a free tune-up and lube job. Since the starlet he was ever hopeful of pretty girls. He grinned at us while we waited just inside the garage door. Time had not been as kind with Vinnie as it had with Eli's Buick. He had been liberated of most of his teeth. The nervous ticks that had given him a comic, visual interest ten or twenty years ago had worn thin on the populace of Taylor. He had been dirty before. Now he was too filthy to contemplate. Only his skill as a mechanic brought people to the garage. Vinnie made out the bill on a slip of paper, using the nose of the Buick as a table. He could just manage a pencil stroke or two before he had to perform some ritual, a combination of harlequin steps, an adjusting of eyebrows and ears, a prodding of orifices. Finally he handed the sheet over to Josie, gave her his gaping grin, and pointed toward the bathroom and the kitchen beyond.

Would you like a cup of coffee?

Josie grinned back at Vinnie.

Tempting, she told him. *Normally I would, but got to get to the courthouse in Parker before five to register the car.* She handed the white slip of paper back to him with a roll of dollars. *You can keep that bill, too, Vinnie. Add it to your collection.*

Thank you, Vinnie crowed and shoved the white paper in his mouth and chewed. The act of chewing stilled his body. He contemplated the ceiling, then pointed. As we watched he formed the chewed paper in his mouth and spat. The spitwad shot up and slapped against the ceiling, joining thousands of others.

That's where I put the ladies, he smiled nostalgically. *They don't always want to stay up there, but don't you worry. I made sure you will. See that one?* he said, pointing to a blackened lump three inches from the new inductee. *That's HER.*

Her?

HER. I put you right next to HER.

Josie's delighted laugh pealed through the empty room and bounced off the smeared walls with their delicate, faded roses. Nervously, I watched for a reaction among the spitwads that hung like thousands of loosened teeth.

I'm honored, Vinnie. Thank you.

Josie pulled up in front of Gram's, gave the horn two short honks and then slid her hands lovingly across the polished dashboard, the steering wheel, the seat.

What took you so long? Carrie and my cousins chorused as they jumped into the car.

I was being placed into the firmament of Vinnie's heaven, Josie told them.

Mystified, they turned to me.

She has her own wad on the ceiling. She's right up there

192

next to HER.

Carrie whistled. Paul put on his most brotherly voice.

Josie, you didn't go into that kitchen, did you?

Josie looked over her shoulder at Paul and smiled her Cheshire Cat smile.

I didn't have to.

In the front seat we had Josie, Carrie, and Aunt Millie's Tiny on my lap. In the back were Paul, Sofie, Marko, Little Sam, Mary Narkovitch, and her cousin Stevo. Josie kept the car in first gear as we roared up Sixth Street. Aunt Anna came out wiping her hands on her apron and glowering. We felt safe, a tight-packed humanity within the steel shell of Josie's car. As we giggled, Josie revved the engine, tooted her horn, and waved to her mom like a beauty queen. At the end of Sixth Street she turned onto Highway 50 and headed out of town.

Okay, let's see what this baby can do, she murmured.

We held our breath as she clutched and shifted into second gear. The car revved briefly, the gears catching, and we surged forward smoothly.

That's right, Josie purred to the car. *How do you like your first taste of second gear? Want to try third? I knew you would!*

We were on our way.

In front of the Parker Court House, we tumbled out of the car and stood around complaining of each other's sharp knees and elbows.

Stay out here, Josie told us bluntly. She smoothed her hair and headed toward the courthouse door.

Sofie pulled a deck of cards from her back pocket. We sat on the courthouse steps and began a game of seven-card stud, twos, and one-eyed jacks wild. Sofie lent us money from her burgeoning pockets.

I won't charge interest. If you win anything, you can keep it, she offered magnanimously. *But only after you pay me back the original loan.*

We had time for five hands while Josie smooth-talked the registrar into putting the car into her name instead of Eli's without so much as a pink slip. The sun had sunk behind the tailings piles, and we were sitting in blue shadows before she came out.

Mine, was all she said.

Must have been a man, Carrie commented to me.

Josie smiled.

She took us to the Nevada Hotel for dinner. A woman with her own car didn't hang out in corner drug stores. She sailed through the ground floor casino and up the center of the wide staircase. We struggled to keep up, clustering together and looking around, quietly and a little in awe. The Nevada Hotel was nowhere near as big and flashy as the joints in Reno or Elko, but it sure wasn't Taylor, either. Everyone who worked there seemed to be aware of that, too.

I'm not sure we have a table, the hostess said with a tight smile.

The dining room was empty.

Look again, Josie said, smiling back.

Aunt Millie's Tiny stuck her thumb in her mouth. Mary Narkovitch tugged at Josie's elbow and urged, *Let's go, Josie.*

Josie was immovable. The hostess sighed, counted us twice, as if our sheer magnitude could hardly be comprehended and then led us to a table in the corner by the swinging kitchen door. She slapped down our menus and escaped contagion in the kitchen.

Isn't this nice, Josie smiled at us.

We blinked back.

What will we have? Burgers and shakes? What do you want, Tiny?

Aunt Millie's Tiny whimpered, rubbed her nose along her arm, and stared at her upside-down menu.

Can't she read yet? The waitress was back at Josie's elbow.

A pencil was stuck in her tall, conical hairdo. Behind her the kitchen door swung fitfully in and out.

She's only five, Sofie explained.

She looks twice that. You people grow 'em big.

Silently, I agreed with her. My legs were still smarting from the ride to Parker. But from Josie, there was an almost imperceptible stiffening.

I think we'll have the special.

One special to share? The waitress pulled the pencil from her hairdo. We watched, fascinated to see if the hairdo could stand unaided.

No, Josie corrected her. *We'll each have the special. With milkshakes.*

Our eyes swiveled to Josie.

Chocolate, I think.

Our eyes returned to the waitress.

So, I have ten, the waitress emphasized. *Ten T-bone specials with chocolate shakes. Anything else?*

We looked at Josie.

Pie. Apple.

Sofie's jaw dropped. The waitress turned her back and headed for the kitchen.

Oh, Waitress, Josie called. *The hotel does make their apple pie with fresh apples? Not canned?*

The kitchen door swung wildly.

Carrie disappeared before dessert, while the dinner plates were being cleared away. After five minutes Josie and I exchanged a look. I went to go get her. It was dark outside and cool. The sounds of the casino drifted out onto the street and followed me the three blocks to the truncated, unnamed street where the whorehouses were. Carrie was sitting on the curb watching the white clapboard house. Jazz blared from the buildings, a different tune from each. Parked cars reflected the bright lights from the windows. The Divine's window at the

Green Willow was darker, flickering in golden tones.

I tried to go in, she said, somehow knowing I was the one standing behind her. *The bouncer wouldn't let me. He said, 'Get the hell away kid. Unless you're looking for a job.'*

There was a burst of laughter like machine gun fire from The Yum Yum Tree. Tunes changed. A blue car pulled up, parked. Two high school boys in athletic jackets jumped out laughing, and, slapping each other on the back, headed for Number 45.

So, I thought I'd just sit here for a while.

The Divine's window continued to glow, lit by some interior combustion. I sat down next to Carrie and joined in the watching. Another ten minutes passed before Josie's car slid to a stop next to us.

Get in, five voices from the back urged us nervously.

The police are after us, Aunt Millie's Tiny told us seriously.

Hardly, Josie said tersely.

Once in the front seat, we executed a turn in front of the whorehouses and peeled off. The interior of the car felt extra full with tight, stiff bodies and the added weight of a heavy silence. Safely out of Parker, Paul finally leaned forward.

We didn't have enough to pay the bill, Paul told us.

A dollar thirty-two short, added Little Sam.

And no tip, said Stevo.

The waitress wouldn't let us send back the two pieces of pie, Mary Narkovitch said.

Sofie held up a bag. *We brought them with us.*

We would have made it except for the pie, Paul added mournfully.

But still no tip, repeated Stevo.

She didn't deserve a tip, Josie's voice was sharp with annoyance, at us, at herself.

We stared at her, our silence weighted with reproach and guilt. We were a family of generous tippers, all of Sixth Street was. You never bought what you couldn't afford. You never stiffed another working man. It was the golden rule. Even Josie followed it.

I'm keeping the pie, Sofie said suddenly, defensively. *I had to chip in my whole winnings. It's the most expensive pie I'll ever eat.*

What about the police? Aunt Millie's Tiny asked in a small, regretful voice. She had been hoping for a high-speed chase, perhaps a shoot-out.

They're not getting my pie! muttered Sofie.

There are no police, Tiny, I whispered to her and settled her more comfortably on my lap.

The rest of the road to Taylor was traveled in a silence soon punctuated by Tiny's soft snores.

The new sheriff flashed his lights at us as we rounded the corner at Mrs. Miniverri's In-home Diner. He had acquired the habit of stalking the diner, watching the silent crowds slip in and out. He was biding his time, waiting for Johnny to reappear.

As she pulled to the curb, Josie checked her watch.

It's past curfew, her voice low and tense.

The new sheriff walked over and shined his light in, picking out each of our faces.

It's past curfew, he said.

His light was full in Josie's face. Her lashes made spiky black peaks across her brow.

Just, she countered softly, sweetly.

Get out, the new sheriff said coldly. *All of you.*

Aunt Millie's Tiny moaned as I shifted to open the door.

What is it? she mumbled around her thumb.

The police, I whispered, jockeying her from the car.

I knew it, she said in a tired, satisfied voice.

He lined us up on the sidewalk and strolled along us, sniffing the air around us for the hint of alcohol, flashing his light in each of our faces in turn. Aunt Millie's Tiny shivered in the clutches of incipient confession. I put my arm around her and squeezed, willing her to silence. The new sheriff's light hesitated on me, then slid past Sofie, who clutched her bag of mangled apple pie to her chest. The light passed Little Sam, Mary Piscovitch, Stevo, Paul, and stopped on Carrie.

Ain't you that whore's daughter?

Yes, Carrie whispered thickly, cleared her throat, said again, *Yes.*

Uh-huh, he said as Carrie blinked into the light.

I was too far along the line. I couldn't take her hand, squeeze her finger tightly.

Her father's the town doctor, I said.

There was a small intake of breath along the line, but the new sheriff didn't even look in my direction.

It is past curfew, Josie's voice was a new thing, tentative, conciliatory, uncertain. *Won't you let me take them home?*

The flashlight swung towards Josie, pinning her in the darkness. I could feel the effort it took her not to blink. Aunt Millie's Tiny snuffled against my waist.

The flashlight snapped off.

Get back to where you belong, he said, his voice like a slap coming at us in the sudden blackness.

We stood there and took it, even Josie. We had already gambled and spent all we had. The sheriff turned and walked back to his car. Josie drove everyone home, her movements stiff and jerky. There was no need to urge silence about what happened. The entire evening was trapped inside us.

When the car at last came to a stop in front of Gram's, Josie rested her head against the steering wheel. I got out of the car, came around, and opened her door.

Let's go to bed, Mala, she said, stepping out of the car.

You just called me Mala, Josie.

Josie shrugged her shoulders, pushed her hair back from her face in a slow, tired raking of her fingers.

That's who you are. Mala. I never could get anyone to call you Becky, except Mimi and Kiki. The effort put them in a terrible tizzy. Josie paused and smiled sadly at the thought.

Together we watched the night sky hung between the branches of the cottonwood tree in Gram's front yard.

She sighed, *Nothing ever changes around here. All you can do is get away.*

It's okay. I don't mind being Mala. I always was, I told her. *And what you said's not true, Josie. Look at today,* I pointed out, trying to coax that cat's grin to her shadowed face, trying to win back my Josie. *Something did change. Remember? You were enshrined on Vinnie Barbarini's ceiling. You're right up there next to HER.*

Her smile hung for an instant in the gloom between us and disappeared, a ghost. She reached out in the darkness and put her arm around me.

Something did change, Josie murmured, drawing me toward the house.

23

We were climbing. Straight above, the sun pressed a hot hand on the top of my head, my shoulders, the bulging string bag on my back. The heat had not yet reached the deep blue hollows along the cliff face where the rock still exhaled a cool last breath before inhaling and holding the heat of the day. Soon only the lizards, with tender bellies the color of evening sky, would find relief in cramped spaces beneath the boulders on the trail. I heard Carrie slip behind me.

Jeez, this is tough, she muttered. *Hold up for a minute.*

I gained level ground and stood up to wait for her. The weight of the bag dragged at my shoulders; I took it off and set it in the shade of the cliff. Gram's plates gave a disapproving clunk. Carrie scrabbled up next to me and stood puffing and pushing sweaty curls from her forehead. She looked at the trail sweeping away below us and Taylor, further still, dusty and noisy, nervous with activity in the noonday sun.

Wow. Hello down there, Carrie hollered breathlessly and laughed. *This is quite the climb.* She eyed the cliff face over her shoulder.

It's worth it. Come on. I shouldered my bag and started up the path again.

At the top, Carrie dropped her sack unceremoniously. Coke bottles escaped from their blanket wrappings and clinked against each other. Carrie twirled, taking in the view on all sides.

This is amazing! Look, you can see Mt. Wheeler.

We stood watching the snow glitter on top of the distant peak.

There's more snow than there was a few days ago, I told her. I looked at the far mountain and thought about the bristlecones facing another winter.

She watched me.

How often do you come up here?

Not very often, I said quickly, defensively.

Carrie's black eyebrows rose.

Every few days or so, I admitted. *Lately...*

Like your mom.

No.

Carrie was silent.

I tried to explain. *Josie's stuff is scattered all over Gram's... what she's taking... what she's not taking... And it's nice up here, and... It's not about my... I gave all that up.*

A dimple twitched in Carrie's cheek. She grinned, *Yah, so did I.*

Well, maybe a little about her, I admitted. *This was her place.*

That's okay, she shrugged. *Proximity,* she formed the word with precise, red lips.

What?

Proximity. It's being close to something. Or someone. It's my new word.

Proximity, I echoed, feeling the weight of the word on my tongue, its taste, its tart justice. Carrie sitting on the curb, looking across the no-name street at a pair of flicking, golden windows was proximity, as close as she could get.

Proximity, I said again.

That's it, Carrie nodded decisively. *Now let's eat!*

We spread the blanket at the edge of the cliff, Taylor and the pale, toxic Sands at our toes, Mt. Wheeler a distant backrest. We scooped out cold, hard dirt and put two Coke bottles in the deep shade beneath a boulder and brought two back to the blanket. Out of my bag I pulled two plates, two forks, two paper napkins, and two of Eli's Ball jars filled with a chunky, gray mass. Carrie suspiciously eyed the Ball jars.

What is that stuff?

Lunch.

I know, but what is it?

Lamb salad. It's pieces of leftover lamb roast. See. We had leftover lamb, but it tastes too strong on the second day, so I marinate it in wine vinegar and olive oil, red onions, some herbs, salt, pepper... and garlic, of course.

Of course. Is it edible? That's all I want to know.

Trust me. You'll love it. Besides, anybody who eats scrambled eggs with hot dogs can't be too picky.

True, Carrie laughed, blushing.

I pulled out a hunk of leftover bread from breakfast and two pieces of rhubarb pie, each neatly wrapped in a dishtowel.

A feast! she cried and whipped a bottle opener out of the back pocket of her trousers.

You should have brought some of Eli's wine.

We'd never make it back down alive.

We'd have to live up here!

We sat and grinned at each other.

I ladled lamb salad on to the plates and tore the bread in half. We ate in silent enjoyment and mopped up our plates with the bread.

Pie now?

Later. I'm stuffed, Carrie groaned and flopped back on the blanket.

It's great here, she sighed. *We should have brought our swimsuits. You can lay out up here and not even get hot, the breeze is so cool.*

It's high.

It sure is that. Carrie turned over on her stomach, her head at the edge of the cliff. I joined her. Chins on our arms, we watched the valley below.

It's like flying without leaving the ground, she said and reached her arms out over empty space.

I pulled her arms back. *It's not flying, then.*

She shrugged her shoulders and yawned, *Nap time. Let's take a snooze.*

I woke around two. I could measure the time by the post

office flag below me. It had swung around and now pulled fitfully toward southeast, its wire twanging against the hollow metal pole. The rest of the town was hushed, waiting. In the far northwest the pale line of hills had disappeared, blotted out in a brownish gray nothing that hung between the blue of the sky and the cracked whiteness of The Sands. I shook Carrie.

Look, I pointed.

My gosh, she murmured, watching the dust storm advance toward Taylor.

It's scarier from up here, she whispered, as if it were a monster whose attention she might attract and so set it on us.

In silence we watched Gram's house swallowed, then Aunt Anna's, then all of Sixth Street, then Main. The dust crept up the streets toward the smelter and the cliff. The post office flagpole banged furiously somewhere, its sound muted by the thick air.

Do you think it'll reach here? Carrie asked nervously, inching back from the edge.

No. We're too high, I reassured her.

We watched the liquid, brown air boil against the base of the cliffs. The tip of the smelter smokestack stuck up above the dust like a reed in a dirty pond, in another spot, the slender needle of the Mormon Church, further on the cross of the Church That Was Not Mormon and Was Not Catholic, and at the northern reach of town, the upper edge of the ballpark scoreboard. Everything else was gone.

Well, Carrie said finally, in her voice the brink of surprise, perhaps relief. *I guess that takes care of Taylor.... Let's have that pie!*

She retrieved the last two bottles of Coke, and I unwrapped the wedges of pie, used one of the dishtowels to polish the plates and forks, and set a piece of pie on each plate.

This is great pie, Carrie managed around a mouthful. *I just don't get how you make all this stuff.*

Gram, I said.

I sat remembering. Gram's hands shaping the bread. Gram's face over a pot of soup, a sizzling roast, carefully sniffing, testing with quick fingers, tasting, adding what was missing. Gram's arms around me in the kitchen after a day at school. *Mala! Mala! You back! I so hungry for you all day!*

I guess it's like having a mom, picking things up from them, Carrie said, breaking my reverie.

I nodded, *Proximity...*

What kind of tips do you think I could pick up from my mom? Carrie grinned briefly; her dimple appeared, quivered, was gone. She looked down at the narrow ridge of piecrust in her hand, her hair falling forward, ruffled by the breeze, hiding her face.

Something, Carrie. She took care of you when you were a baby, for a while, maybe... She could teach you something.

Carrie sighed, *Well, you're right about that.* She jumped to her feet.

This is for you, Sheriff! She sent the crust sailing out over the cliff, arcing down into the dust.

Hey! Don't waste my pie crust!

Carrie laughed, bent, scooped up a handful of rocks. I jumped to join her. We flung rocks out over the cliff, enumerating every enemy in town—watchful, suspicious merchants, snippy, self-righteous uptown ladies, their torturing, vengeful kids. The rocks flew like spiteful birds. Somewhere down in the murky dust storm, we imagined them connecting. A considerable patch of ridge was cleaned of debris before we were done. Then we explored. I showed Carrie the bootlegger's blackened cave. I told her about my dad and uncle carting buckets of whiskey down the cliff as kids, giving it to Gram to bottle and sell. We searched the cave for the bootlegger's bones.

Carried off by coyotes, Carried sighed, and brushed her dirty hands on her pants.

I didn't show her the cave with the drawings and bits of ancient pots, even though I knew she wouldn't tell. The memory of Uncle Nick's gently urgent hand as he pulled my fingers back, his reverent steps, his words were etched in my mind more deeply than the restless, flowing design on the flickering wall. Fragile secrets that proximity could destroy.

We climbed back to the ridge and packed up and sat with our feet dangling over the cliff, watching the wind die and the dust settle, Taylor emerging, dirty and unchanged. Slowly, people stepped out of buildings and shook themselves off, men from the Taylor Club and pool hall to stretch and breathe before returning for one more, shop owners to sweep doorsteps, women to rehang still-wet laundry, children, like balls hurtling from cannon, free to play.

Everyone's so small. I can blot them out with a finger. Carrie stuck out her thumb and sighted it judiciously. *Oops, there goes Mr. Peterings. Who will make sure I don't swipe any penny candy now? Oh-oh, there goes Lyle Linden and his brand new bike. Sorry Lyle.*

Look, I pointed. *Another moving van.*

I sighted with my thumb and blocked it out.

Well, the Radocovitches won't be moving. I just erased their van.

The Radocovitch's moving van made three in town in one day, two on Sixth Street, one out in Irish Town—-a dirt road with four company houses clustered at the far edge of the ball park and everyone with the last name of Murphy. Tiny men were busy hauling out doll furniture and inching it up the precarious ramps in the backs of the vans. The vans were too scattered to block them all out with my fingers. No matter how I spread my hands, one always slipped through.

Everybody's leaving, I murmured.

We watched the march of men, the parade of household goods trailing out of box houses and into vans. Kids on bikes sailed past, skidded into sharp turns, and pedaled back to watch. Carrie sighed.

We might be leaving... she admitted quietly.

The sounds of the town drifted up to us.

No, I told her.

My dad's been looking at trade magazines. At the jobs. Has he said anything?

Carrie shook her head, her curls swinging like heavy bells. *He never says anything. I just see him looking, sometimes circling with a pen... .*

But why? He doesn't want to leave! He's been waiting so long.

I think he thinks we should... Carrie whispered. *For me... .*

I looked at her, looked away. *You told him!* I accused. *You told him about going to see her again. You told him about what the new sheriff said!*

I tell him everything, Mala. He's my dad.

But, Carrie! I protested.

Carrie sat quietly, looking out over the town. *You know, every day he looks at me and sees her. We both want her back, but he wants something else, too, Mala. He wants me to be different...to be 'not her'. I have to do that, too.* She whispered, *I didn't really understand that until that night, after we came home from Parker, after we ran into the new sheriff.*

It's a lot, I said. *That damn new sheriff...*

Carrie shrugged, *It's the way things are, Mala, that's all.*

You sound like Josie. You sound like you want to go, too, Carrie.

No. I'd stay, but maybe it would be better for him. I'd wait. You can never tell. She might... Carrie's voice slipped away over the cliff.

She stood up, brushed the dirt from her pants.

We should get going, she said.

We packed quietly, thoughtfully. She hefted her bag on her shoulder. I hesitated.

Aren't you coming?

No, I shook my head. *I want to stay a bit longer. Maybe wait for the sunset.*

Well, he'll be waiting for me…

It's okay. You should go.

Carrie walked to the edge of the trail. I watched her black curls disappear over the cliff. I ran to the edge.

Carrie, I called.

She looked up.

Carrie. Everybody says you look just like her.

Below me, Carrie waited. I watched her black brows contract. I took a deep breath.

But, well, you're like him, too. More like him. All the best parts. Like him.

Her face lit into a smile, the dimple deep and strong. We smiled at one another in the angled glow of the sinking sun.

You know, she said finally, grinning now, *If we do go, Dad and I, maybe she'll follow us! In a new place it could be different.*

I nodded. *If I was her, I would follow you,* I told her.

I know you would! she laughed and turned and left me.

I returned to the spot at the cliff and watched Carrie's hesitant progress as she negotiated boulders and switchbacks, minute by minute moving closer to her home. I watched the lengthening shadows stretch cool, blue fingers over the white-hot Sands and slip over Taylor. Below, a flurry of final activities eddied through town. Moving van doors were closed, locked as if their contents were gold; men stepped from the Taylor Club and weaved home toward dinner. I saw Uncle Nick close up the barbershop. He stopped in front of Milan's and waited without knocking. Milan stepped out of his shoe repair shop, and in a companionable silence I could hear from my cliff top, they headed toward Anna's. Behind them, the barber pole, red white, red white, slowly wound to a stop.

Carrie was right. They were so small. My uncles marched like tiny, solemn soldiers. Aunt Anna worked noisily in her doll's kitchen, waiting to gather her men and children around her. Mimi & Kiki, like miniature birds, chirped somewhere in their little house at the far end of Sixth Street. Even Josie was reduced, prowling, wondering, *Where's my dinner?* So small, fragile as bits of pottery. From up here, I could cup my whole family in my palm, hold the whole town in my two hands. My hands were strong now. I had kneaded bread every morning at dawn for months. I had done laundry and dishes, cleaned the house, worked the garden. Since Gram died. I could do it, hold them, protect them. I could reach an arm across thirty miles and with two fingers pluck a beautiful whore from amongst her admirers and carry her back, her arms and legs wheeling in air, and give her, a brightly-wrapped trinket from heaven, to my tiny, yearning friends. From up here, I could gather them all close. I could keep them from leaving.

The sun was dropping behind the far hills without the brilliance of an accompanying sunset; only Mt. Wheeler burned with the departing light, its snowy peak a candle in the east. No ghost rose from the warm dirt around me to lift me and carry me out over the cliff. I was alone. I stood and shouldered my bag and started down. In Gram's house, spaghetti was waiting to be boiled, meat sauce to be heated, lettuce to be washed and torn and placed in the glass bowl, tossed with the dressing I had already made. Josie was waiting, waiting for dinner.

Taylor was dark by the time I reached it, lit only by the bright beacons of kitchen windows, and in a few uptown houses by the new television sets that blinked in shades of gray. I cut through the alley behind C Street and stopped opposite the new sheriff's back yard. The picket fence, newly painted, glowed in the gloom. The kitchen window framed a neighborly church lady, intent on dishes. In the yard, the new sheriff's son, legs straining toward the pale stars, rode a swing. Chains creaking, poles groaning, the swing carried him, laughing, up and up. On the far side of the alley, I wrapped my arms around an old cottonwood and watched from the dark.

Higher, Daddy! Higher!

Blacker than the surrounding night, the new sheriff stood behind his boy, his fedora on the trimmed grass beside him. He smiled, his teeth glowing white as the picket fence. He pushed gently, stepped back, and watched his boy's flight.

Higher! Higher! the boy laughed and urged the swing upward with his whole body.

The man laughed, too, stepped forward to meet the swing, and pushed with a steady, well-practiced movement. His arms remained outstretched for a moment, urging, protective, still claiming connection.

How's that, Son!

Whoopee! I'm on top of the world, Daddy! Again, Daddy! Higher! I want to go higher!

Okay! Here you go!

From my cliff top, I could have rubbed the new sheriff out, erased him with a slight pressure of my thumb. The surging child laughed, was pushed again by the father, arched upward, his path across the sky marked by a momentary darkening of the stars.

I felt the rough bark of the cottonwood against my cheek and blinked at the wavering vision. I thought of the cottonwood's downy offspring, that flowing, white column rising around Gram's casket. The cottonwood trees, anchored in a swirling, dancing river of their children. Two months ago, you could have gathered handfuls, lifted them up, blown softly, and watched them fly. It would be hard to find a single seed now. Scattered.

Gram was gone. Josie was going, Carrie, too. One seed was all I needed, one seed saved from the masses that had been caught, crushed under foot, or carried off, one seed to plant and care for, one seed that was mine.

24

No one had ever walked across The Sands. There were dangers: tiny, white scorpions and pale, misshapen rattlesnakes. These, the only creatures that lived on the cracked wastes of The Sands, had absorbed into their bodies all the evil effluents of our world. The toxic slag from the smelter flowed out onto The Sands and with it the sewage of Taylor. Occasional nuclear bomb tests deposited their radiant dust there. The scorpions and the rattlesnakes on The Sands were ten times as poisonous, ten times as ornery. That's what the mothers of Taylor said.

DON'T GO OUT ON THE SANDS, the mothers said.

The reservation was on the far side, about twenty houses backed against the hills with their faces toward our common wasteland. The hundred or so people of the reservation claimed one pickup truck, two hundred square miles of non-arable land, one deep well for their makeshift homes and for their livestock, and the right to pick any pinyon pine nut in the state. Pine nuts kept them alive. Water would have made their lives easier. Sal had gone down swinging in that battle decades ago, and no one had taken up the fight.

People from Taylor didn't go out onto The Sands. They didn't go to the reservation. So that's where I decided to go. Choosing what to take was easy: a few clothes, my winter coat, my favorite iron pan, and all of Gram's handkerchiefs, one hundred, each embroidered with its own delicate, long-remembered wildflower from eastern Europe. I held them to my nose. Yes, they smelled of Gram. I would take the small stack of government checks in their brown envelopes that had accumulated on my chest of drawers since Gram's death, checks from the Veteran's Administration, from Social Security. I would take Johnny Miniverri. He would be my cottonwood seed. I would save him. He would save me.

I imagined slipping in through Mrs. Miniverri's unlocked front door, negotiating the tables in the dark front room, rousing Johnny from his bed or his closet, offering him my hand, and leaving. I could count on his silence. I would take him as he was, carry his shoes until I could safely help him put them on, buy whatever else he needed later. We would walk straight out across The Sands, and on the other side they would be waiting for us. The sun would just be coming up behind the far cliffs, my mother's cliffs. I would carry with me the finished story of Naked Sal. They would recognize us as pilgrims. They would welcome us. We could pay our own way. I would help pick pine nuts. I would make bread. In some quiet spot among them, untroubled by smelter whistles, passed over by howling dust storms, no longer stalked, Johnny Miniverri would crack wide open, like a pine cone in the sun. The kernel would emerge, a young man who had once tasted of honey and cinnamon. I would take care of him. *My* family.

It didn't work that way.

Johnny Miniverri was not sleeping peacefully in his bed. He was in his closet with his blanket wrapped securely around his head. At first I thought he might have suffocated, he was so still, but as I unwrapped him, he began to struggle. We fought in slow motion, bumping cautiously against the padded, close walls. Two people desperate to win as quietly as possible. I was the more determined, the more desperate. Sitting tangled in the blanket, breathing heavily, we watched each other, I willing his understanding, he waiting for feared words. I took his hand and we just sat there. I could feel the minutes crowding with us in the tight, dark space of the closet.

I'm going to take you to a quiet place, my voice so low it was more a vibration inside me than actual words.

He flinched, watched the words invade the air around his head. He ducked and bobbed as if attacked.

Holding his hand, I stood and pulled him to his feet. He still clutched the corner of his blue blanket, so I wrapped it

211

around him and wordlessly coaxed him out of his closet, out of his room, out of his house. I sat him on the front porch, went back inside to retrieve shoes and socks for him, my suitcase waiting for me on the floor at the end of his bed. On the way out, I set a thin envelope on one of the felt tabletops. He sat in his blanket and watched me as I rolled socks up his unresisting feet, my movements slow and soundless. I slipped his shoes on his feet and tied the laces as if any careless twitch or tug would cause the brown oxfords to explode in my fingers. I gathered two pairs of Mrs. Miniverri's red and white slippers from beside the front door. We wore them over our shoes. Not even the sound of our shoes on the sidewalk would mark our passage out of Taylor. Taking his hand in mine, we walked down the street and crossed Main. I guided him through the side yards of houses heavy with sleep, across Sixth Street, around the yard of Bearded Maria's shack and out onto the flat, cracked plate of The Sands. The stars were blue, pale and distant, the dark hills a low, sinuous line. Not a single light beckoned us. Ten miles of walking, three hours till dawn. We could make it.

About half way, when The Sands seemed to stretch indefinitely in every direction, to travel with us, trapping us at its heart, Johnny stopped. I tugged at his arm, wordlessly motioning ahead. He ignored me, pulled his arm away, and stood so still it seemed even his heart had obliged him and paused in its beating.

I hear the earth rotating, he breathed. *I hear gravity.*

I listened. Overcome with a sudden dizziness, I checked the ground beneath me. Below my feet, two white scorpions explored a deep crack in the kilned earth. Gathering into themselves the available light, they glowed dimly.

I tugged on Johnny's arm, urging movement.

Johnny took a step, reaching his left foot out with wobbling uncertainty, setting it down slowly, hesitantly, gingerly testing the earth. His arms reached out for balance, the blanket unfurling, fledgling wings. He took another painstaking step.

We were almost across when the snake struck. Its pale, mottled body invisible in the sickly, gray dust, it lay flat and stretched out, collecting the last leaking heat from the ground. Johnny had been wise to step carefully. There was no warning rattle like they tell you, no coiling, no rising, swaying display of power. Just a quick, liquid stir of dust and strike and a slipping, fluid escape. Then pain. I looked at my calf in wonder. Heat gathered there. I moaned. Johnny moaned, too, and dipped his head, wrapping blue wool wings around, sealing himself inside. I pressed my lips together and, shaking violently, I succumbed to gravity and sank. There was a great roaring in my ears. I could hardly form thought in its rush of noise.

I hear it, too, Johnny, I informed him. I was surprised at how deafening it was, how easily recognizable. *Johnny... I'm bitten. I hear it now. So loud. But, we can't stop for it. We have to keep going....*

The blue cocoon swayed slightly away from me, balancing on the spinning plate of The Sands.

Gram, I called out this one word, sent it out across the wasteland to do battle with gravity, a talisman, a longing, a farewell.

Next to me, the cocoon trembled as if in a breeze.

I tried to tether my thoughts to the swirling heat and pain in my leg. Venom. There was anti-venom. Looking over my shoulder, I thought, *back there.* A few early lights twinkled along Sixth Street, old ladies making the morning loaf. The cliffs behind town were black and solid against an eastern sky opal with approaching dawn. Eight, eight and a half miles. Ahead of us I could see the sage-rubbled edge of The Sands, beyond, the graying lift of hills, between, the scattered, squat houses of the reservation. There, too, a few lights were coming on. Standing, the earth veered beneath me again, but I clawed at the air and balanced and won. I picked up our suitcase and hopped to Johnny. Carefully, slowly, I unwrapped him.

213

Johnny, I murmured, choosing my words carefully. *Carry me.*

He watched my lips, watched the words form and expand, disturbing the predawn air. He shuddered and ducked. I held him there next to me, pointed to the swelling leg, to the reservation.

Carry me.

He did.

They waited at the edge of The Sands, watching our progress, two men with rifles and a woman, short, round, and red-aproned, her arms folded across her chest. We were not pilgrims. We were strangers, trouble, two dusty white people, wrapped in a blue blanket, one carrying the other, the other carrying a suitcase, both inexplicably wearing dusty slippers over their shoes. As we stepped off The Sands, they assessed our situation. In silence they lifted me from Johnny's arms, left him to pull the blanket once again tightly around himself. In silence, they shepherded us both to the community truck and settled me in the rusted truck bed in loose hay, Johnny and his blanket in the cab. We left the reservation, and carrying the silence with us, returned to Taylor.

25

I was lucky. That's what Carrie's father said as he put the needle to my arm. My skin resisted, retreating, denting in deeper and deeper, fighting the point, losing the battle, giving up. Dr. Price gently extracted the needle, laid it aside, and reached for another.

For the pain, he told me.

This time my skin did not resist.

Doesn't look too bad, he said, prodding the darkened skin around the wound on my calf. *Typically you'll see this blackening, but more extensive. And we can still bend your knee a bit. See? That's good...must not have injected too much venom when it struck. Very lucky,* he said again.

From across the empty ward a sudden, tremendous snort echoed. The Methodist-Minister-Without-a-Flock rolled over on his back in the farthest bed. His right hand fell off his chest to hang limply from the bed. His chest slowly expanded with air, stopped at its apex, held for a moment. He gargled, snorted, and exhaled noisily to begin the process anew. Dr. Price smiled.

Tied one on last night in Parker. He comes here to sleep it off. Lost everything at craps...again.

He always loses, I informed the doctor. *He's not very good.*

The doctor said, *Oh, I don't know about that. Miss Amelia will be here later on to pick him up. She takes him home, cleans him up, feeds him. I think our Methodist Minister has a convert.*

The Methodist-Minister-Without-a-Flock choked and sputtered, unaware that he was lucky, even luckier than I.

Anyway, Carrie's father sighed, *he shouldn't bother you too much. The shot will help. Get some rest.*

Still he stood, forgetting me, and watched the drunken minister, jealously almost, until he shook himself, shrugged his bent shoulders, and left the room.

I wasn't allowed to sleep. Word had spread. Since the pick-up truck, driven by the silent woman in her red apron, had arrived at the clinic with its burden of two dusty white people, word had spread. Carrie escorted the truck to Mrs. Miniverri's to drop off Johnny and the blanket, then she pointed the way to Gram's house, where Carrie and my suitcase disembarked. The pickup truck sped off. On her way home, Carrie passed the word along Sixth Street, dropped in at the shoe shop, the barbershop, and the Taylor Club and spread the word along Main through clusters of women.

They came in two and threes, in small groups of bristling black wool and matching black shoes, or in faded summer dresses with light sweaters. No one came empty-handed. Down on Sixth Street, the sick and the sad needed only two things to recover: company and a little gift.

Aunts Mimi and Kiki were the first. They came scurrying in, to perch on the bed next to me, their shoulders and hips touching, black shiny purses in laps, twin hairdos trembling. They brought a slice of white cake with frosting the warm yellow color of a baby chick.

Mala, we're so glad you're back. Aren't we, Mimi?

Yes, Kiki. So glad!

Just as glad as can be!

Yes!

Yes...well...

They exchanged nervous peeks at one another, blinking.

And she brought Johnny back with her! That was good, don't you think, Kiki?

Oh yes, Mimi. Bringing Johnny back was good. That was a good thing to do, Mala. They smiled at me proudly, as if they have heard an entirely different story of my night's work.

But..., I begin.

Twin hairdos shook vigorously.

216

You just lay there and rest, Mala.

Yes, Kiki you're right. Mala, you rest. We'll just sit here, quietly.

Quietly as a mouse... two mice. Won't we, Mimi?

Sometimes, Kiki, mice can be pretty noisy.

Kiki looked at her sister, shocked. *Mimi, when has a mouse been noisy?*

Remember the nest of mice in Lubo Dundervich's chicken coop when we were little? Those mice were noisy.

Mimi. That was fifty years ago.

They were noisy mice, Kiki.

They're not noisy now, Mimi.

Mimi and Kiki stared at each other in impasse. Bright black eyes blinked. They were quiet.

Uncle Nick and Milan were standing hesitantly in the doorway to the ward. Mimi and Kiki fluttered their fingers. Uncle Nick and Milan shuffled in. Uncle Nick slid a thin white paper packet onto the nightstand by the bed, a new comb. Milan leaned over me, fashioned the air with thick, stained fingers.

I make shoes for you, I make 'um strong. Walk anywhere. You see. Good shoes. He nodded his head, smiled, sat down next to Kiki to catch his breath after so many words. Uncle Nick was still standing, his restless eyes traveling around the room.

I went to the cliff to look for you when Mrs. Miniverri called. I thought you might go there.

Too close, I shook my head.

Uncle Nick nodded, understanding. *Never went that direction. Out on The Sands. What's it like out there?*

It's empty, Uncle Nick, I told him. *And wide. And so quiet you can hear—*

Uncle Nick nodded, his eyes strayed east.

With a great eruption of movement and sound, Aunt Anna charged in, Sofie, Paul, Luke and Aunt Millie's Mike, Tiny and

Nicky in her wake. Mimi and Kiki fluttered nervously on their perch. Anna pushed past Uncle Nick and sat on my bed, caught me up, and hugged me tightly.

So thin! she accused harshly.

I've only been gone a few hours, Aunt Anna, I mumbled into her chest.

See!

She glared around the room at Nick, at the clump of gawking children, at Milan, at Mimi and Kiki, quivering on the opposite bed. *How did you all get here so quick?* she demanded.

Milan studied his shoes, Mimi and Kiki blinked rapidly, unable to answer.

Anna, honey, Uncle Nick soothed. *We just came when we heard...*

And we came with you, Ma, Paul explained on behalf of his pack of assembled siblings and cousins. *Remember?*

Aunt Anna snorted.

We brought cake, Mimi squeaked. *Didn't we, Kiki?*

Cake, Kiki's head bobbed, and she gathered Mimi's hand into hers.

Cake! Cake! She doesn't need cake! She needs to be under my roof! That what she needs!

In the wordless wake that always followed one of Aunt Anna's pronouncements, Sofie slipped to my side. She leaned over and whispered.

I'm doing it too, Mala. Next week. Before school starts. I'm running away! She pulled back to give me a significant look, a deep nod. Aunt Anna reached out and smacked her across the head.

Jeez, Ma! Sofie complained, rubbing her head. *What was that for?*

Humph! Aunt Anna glared and pointed a finger at Sofie. *Don't think you can get away with anything under my roof!*

Aw, Ma. You know I'm always good.

Sofie turned her head, winked at me, leaned forward again. *I going to be a riverboat gambler,* she whispered.

I could hear the smile in her voice.

People arrived, aunts and uncles, neighbors, widows tottering on Milan's shoes. Children I had played with, who watched me shyly, asked to touch my leg. Neighbor women made excuses for absent men or presented their husbands, formally, as if I'd never seen them coming home dirty from work, or drunk.

This is my Stanley. Stanley, say hi.... Bob wanted to say how glad he was that you was back. Well, say it, Bob... Your Uncle Sam's still out looking. But he'll be here, if he knows what's good for him...

The men shuffled, mumbled incoherently, backed off, relieved, and joined a growing, jovial group across the room, anchored to the now-awake and sermonizing Methodist Minister. Everyone brought something: soup, loaves of bread, cakes and pies, pre-owned sweaters and slippers in garish party colors, a corduroy robe with a Salt Lake department store's price tag still on it, handmade hankies and doilies, fruit... Aunt Anna became Marshall of the Treasury. Soon, jugs of ice tea circulated, and though it was only noon, jugs of wine and bottles of beer. Dr. Price watched from the door, taking in the scene with his flickering, accepting gaze. Carrie laughed with a group of friends. The widows closed in around me, a solid, soft wall of black. Everyone else gave way. Chairs were dragged forward, a circle formed. They sat with their legs straining their black skirts, their shoes in sturdy, invincible twos, their gnarled fists holding tea or wine. They told me stories of children running away, among them Gram's favorite, the story of my own father's travels to Reno to box in the Golden Gloves. All the stories ended well. They chortled and misted over. Sobering, they recalled their own flights from far-off homes, distant green lands. An argument flared: Which was the hardest place to leave?

I want know something, Mrs. Popodopolous' voice cut through the bristling air. Gesturing hands stilled and dropped. They quieted.

You go Sands, Mala. You tell me. Where all that sand, dust come from? Everyday, wind, dust, no good! I want know where.

I don't know Mrs. Popodopolous. It's empty, I told them, looking around the circle of wrinkled, anxious faces. *It's flat and hard, swept almost.*

Not always like that, Mrs. Pastervich murmured.

The old women looked at her, some nodded.

True. Mister Sal tell story.

No.

Yes. I hear him tell, my kitchen table, long time now.

My kitchen table, too. I hear. Mees Amelia know story.

They turned as one and looked through the milling crowd. There was Miss Amelia, come at last, sitting next to The-Methodist-Minister-Without-a-Flock, holding his hand, listening to his holy tales of gambling. The widows called to her, beckoning her over. She came and sat and smiled shyly around the group.

Mees Amelia, tell story. Tell story of Sands, Mister Sal's story.

Oh, Miss Amelia said, her eyes suddenly sad. *Sal loved that story.*

Tell story, Mrs. Pastervich ordered.

Mrs. Popodopolous nodded. *Mala go there.*

Miss Amelia sighed and thought and began.

It was a story Sal heard from the Indians on the reservation, one of their legends, about the people who settled here first. They called them 'the ancestors'. The ancestors came from the west and traveled a long way searching for a home. When they came into this valley between the hills and the cliffs it was beautiful, green.

See, no always same as now, Mrs. Pastervich interrupted. *Shh...*

Miss Amelia began again. *The Indians told Sal there was a lake, deep and blue, and tall grass. In the hills the pinyons were thick with nuts, and there was plenty of game.*

See!? Mrs. Pastervich burst out.

Shh! The widows roared. *You quiet now. Listen!*

Miss Amelia smiled. *The ancestors had a good life, easy and peaceful. But after they had lived here a long time, a man came, a white man. They had heard stories about the white men, but he came alone, and so they welcomed him, fed him, helped him as he wandered the hills around the valley. He had no interest in the lake, the waving rich grass. He searched for rocks, examined them and placed them in sacks on the back of his mule. Gold, he told them, silver maybe, copper for sure. They didn't know the words. They laughed at him, called him the rock eater. But when he left, they worried. They knew he would be back.*

The widows nodded sadly in unison. Trouble always returned.

The ancestors held a great council. Should they let the rock eaters return? Should they fight? Should they run? For the first time they argued amongst themselves. Their voices became so loud, they made the tall grass bow down and sent ripples across the lake. Their words flew like packs of angry birds, back to the land they had come from. The west wind answered them. The wind blew so long and so hard that the grass dried and turned to dust, the lake disappeared, and the game began to leave. Some of the ancestors left, following the game and living off the pine nuts. Those that stayed prayed for a way to live in their land that was now nothing but a dry desert. The gods listened.

In unison, the widows crossed themselves, pointed to the heavens, then leaned in close, eager as children for the last, best part of the tale.

Just as they had known he would, the prospector returned and many people followed him. It took him a long time to find the valley, it was so changed. He passed through many times before deciding the shape of the dusty hills and cliffs were not lying to him. The lake was gone, the tall grass, too. The land was dry and cracked. And where the people had lived nothing remained but a grove of trees he had never noticed before. Cottonwoods, old and gnarled, desert trees with roots deep in the earth, searching for water.

The widows sighed, satisfied, and sat back.

Mees Amelia, that damn good story.

Sal's story, the Indians' story, she corrected them and stood to return to her Minister.

Still caught in the story, the old women shook their heads at the mystery of it, and sat in a sustained, clouded silence. At last, one of them jabbed a crooked finger toward God, turned the Holy Wheel in the charged air in front of her, and then crossed herself sadly. Soon they were all crossing themselves, nodding with new wisdom.

Sands nogoodgoddam place, one murmured.

Ghosts, agreed another. *That damn wind still angry maybe, too.*

They all nodded. So that was it, I thought. Taylor's Holy Wheel was stuck in history, in sand. We were blasted by it. We were marooned. It explained a lot.

Mala, Mrs. Popodopolous said reverently, taking my hand. *You good, brave girl go Sands. No do that no more.*

I shook my head. I had traveled across The Sands and brought back nothing but the unanswered mystery of the storm and the opportunity for a story. For them it was enough. I was the oracle of the wind. In the future, the widows would weave a fable around me, the fabric of dust.

Josie was the last to come. Ten past three. She parted the crowd without a word, pointed Mario Tantorini out of a chair, and pulled it over to the side of my bed. In the noisy, packed room there was an island of quiet between her chair and my bed, a substantial, cool, uncharted ground. Josie put her purse on the floor and crossed her legs, then her arms.

What a stupid, stupid thing, she informed me tartly.

I looked away. She was right. Worse than a Family Crime.

Next time, don't leave a note.

I was afraid Mrs. Miniverri would worry about Johnny.

She threw up her hands in exasperation, ran her long fingers through her hair, gestured impatiently.

Then why did you take him in the first place? Why didn't you just run away? Just go, get out of here?

I wanted to save him, I said, but I knew that was only partly true. *I wanted...*I whispered. *I just wanted...someone.*

Josie looked down at the hands in her lap. The space between us widened, a continent formed, land masses rose in the silence, mountains, cliffs, impenetrable jungle. Still we moved apart. From a vast distance I watched as Josie finally leaned forward, rifled her purse. She sighed.

I put all your things back, she said into the depths of her purse. She raised her head and looked at me. In her hand were the brown government envelopes.

What are these?

Orphan money. The words felt like hard kernels I had chewed but could not swallow.

She inserted a pale fingernail in one envelope and slit it open, looked in. Her eyebrows rose.

How often do you get these?

Every month. They go into an account, but I didn't know how. Gram always did it. So they just piled up over the summer.

Josie tapped the edge of the envelopes against the palm of her hand. Her eyes were narrowed and thoughtful. She looked over at me. Her smile was a sudden sun over distant hills.

Why did you need so many handkerchiefs? she asked.

I stared at her, couldn't think of the answer, didn't know it.

She laughed suddenly, *That was a hell of a lot of handkerchiefs!* She stood, still laughing, and looked down at me, reached across a world of distance and took my hand.

Look around you, her voice was low. *You're not an orphan.*

They don't understand what I did, Josie.

Of course they do.

She was gone in the crowd. I heard her voice near the door.

Enjoy your welcome home party, Mala!

26

The hand that woke me was abrupt, urgent.

Wake up. Come on.

Josie was standing over me, grasping crutches in one hand. I rubbed my eyes, stared.

Come on. You said you wanted to save him. Get up.

Save who? What's going on?

The new sheriff's at Mrs. Miniverri's. He wants to take Johnny away. Get up.

What? I tangled with the bedclothes.

For kidnapping. And rape.

It had taken a whole day for the word of my nighttime flight across The Sands to break the barrier of Main Street. Now the sheriff had what he needed to lock up Johnny. Josie reached down and ripped the sheet away. I was still in my shirt and skirt, one sock left on my uninjured leg. My skirt was hiked up around my waist, my shirt under my armpits, both a wrinkled, dirty mess. The swelling on my leg had receded to the size of an angry red fist around the black knuckle marks of the bite.

Jesus, you're a mess, Josie commented, annoyed. *It doesn't matter. Come on.* She hauled me out of bed and stuffed the crutches under my arms.

But what can I do? I said, hobbling as fast as I could behind her clicking heels.

We, she corrected me. *I don't know. You stood up to the new sheriff the other night when he stopped us.*

It was dark...

I'll help. We need to do this.

She shoved me into the car, tossed the crutches through the open back window. We roared off. She never shifted. The old car roared along Main in its most familiar gear. People watched and followed. In front of Mrs. Miniverri's a crowd had formed in the yard and along the sidewalk, women and unemployed men from Sixth Street, uptown mothers with their children clustered around them. On the porch, a phalanx of old women, brown grocery bags clutched to chests, stood and glowered. Josie and I shouldered our way through the crowd, stopped at the base of the stairs. The new sheriff stood at the screen door, hands on hips, inside, the shadowy outline of Mrs. Miniverri, pulling on the doorknob, holding it closed.

My boy's a good boy, she insisted softly. She was trying to keep her voice low, to keep the rising panic from reaching like cold, wicked fingers into Johnny's silent space.

I'm taking him, Catherine. Open the door.

On the porch, black sweaters bristled, ruffled like feathers disturbed by the wind.

She no Catherine to you. She Meeses Miniverri, this muttered from somewhere in the back of the clutch of widows. There were nods, grunts of agreement *No-good-god-dam-somabitch,* another mutter, like a low warning growl. The new sheriff rounded on the group of old women.

This is not your business.

Our business. No your business, Mrs. Pastervitch said clearly. The brown paper of her grocery bag crackled in her tightening grip. Behind me, in the yard and along the sidewalk, the crowd gasped, murmured.

A crime's been committed, the sheriff's voice rose. He pointed at the screen door, *I'm locking that crazy bastard up!*

I did it, I heard my voice say. Josie blinked at me, nodded, gave me a slight shove. I hobbled up the stairs and stood in front of the sheriff, alone. His eyes were hidden beneath the tilt of his fedora, his mouth a thin line.

I did it. I kidnapped Johnny, my voice was wobbly, breathless. I cleared my throat, tried to find a human in his face. Not the New Sheriff, just a man, a father. It didn't work. I dropped my eyes. My heart pounded, blood rushed in my ears. Once again I heard the earth's rotation and all the invisible forces that held us here. I focused on the man's Adam's apple, the red, slightly wrinkled skin exposed above the faded collar of his shirt. A tiny razor knick incised a thin, dark line in the hollow below. A pulse beat there. I looked up into his face. Did he see it, too, reflected in my eyes, that vision of a man and a child, a boy who pumped the air and strained forward, a child who wanted to fly? I took a breath.

I kidnapped Johnny. He didn't do anything. He didn't even want to come. I had to drag him out of his house... I thought I could...

The widows crowded around me.

Our business, Mrs. Pastervitch said firmly from behind my left shoulder. *Our town. Our children.*

Beyond the steps, the crowd shuffled and grumbled, even up-town mothers gathered their children closer, nodded. As on the night of the fireworks, we were brought together with a sudden, single emotion. Closer, from behind and around, I heard a rumbling noise, perhaps the murmur of old, gruff voices, perhaps the sound of a wheel, a Holy Wheel, pushed by old hands, breaking loose of its mire and inching forward into America. The sheriff heard it, too. He stepped back, listening.

Shame for you, Mrs. Andopolous, said and shook a finger at the sheriff. The others took up the phrase, *Shame for you. Shame for you.* They placed it in his hands, an offering, like a loaf of newly baked bread, a covered dish redolent with future flavor, a set of matching doilies, or a sweater in loud yarn, knitted just for him. A gift that couldn't be returned. He carried it with him down the stairs and through the parted crowd. *Shame.*

Josie helped me back to the car and stowed the crutches. She sat behind the wheel for a minute.

Well, that worked, she commented dryly.

You were a big help, I told her tartly.

Hey! I got you there. All in all, I think we did a great job, she said with satisfaction.

But, did you see <u>them</u>, Josie? I said proudly. *They were great!*

I was watching you. Josie smiled over at me, started the engine. *This town will be telling stories about you for years. You'll be famous.* She paused and grinned. *Not as famous as me, of course. I'm up on Vinnie Barbarini's ceiling, right next to HER!* Josie's laughter filled the car and launched out the windows, redeemed, released into the clear warm day.

27

I think it was the government checks, those thin, plain brown envelopes with the mottled green slip peeking through the narrow window, the uninteresting typing, my name, Post Office Box, care of Gram. Care of Gram, that wasn't true for me anymore. Sometimes I think it was the thought of me walking across The Sands, the sight of me standing up in front of the sheriff, standing up with my army of widows. I like to think it was that. Knowing Josie, though, it was the checks.

There were pyrotechnics about it, down on Sixth Street, a brilliant, vicious battle between the two most stubborn females in Taylor. The battle drew in first the family, what was left of them, and then the whole street. Lines were drawn, neither side was taking prisoners. In the midst of the battle, Uncle Nick decamped for parts unknown. Reeking of cattle cars and whiskey, he would be back when the air cleared. In the Taylor Club bets were lodged. The tally became so long, and the money held in trust so large, that the bartender took up sleeping on the damp, hard floor behind the bar, loaded shotgun at his side. As Eli's car slowly filled with Josie's possessions, messengers scurried between camps, but it seemed there would be no break in hostilities.

Don't worry, Josie said, luxuriating in the sun at the kitchen table and painting her toenails Vixen Red. Next to her, her cup of coffee and slice of bread sent steaming white flags up into the beams of dusty sun above the table. She put the cup to her lips and blew, dispersing the traitor steam, and sipped. She grinned at me over the rim of her cup, *I'm not above a bit of kidnapping myself.*

Still, I waited. It was the widows who tipped the balance of power. They flocked at Aunt Anna's front gate and entered in mass. I would have never counted on them in this. I must have never really understood them, the way their minds rolled through the world, seeing backwards and forwards, recognizing the roads before they were ever traveled. In their knowing, unhurried way they circumnavigated Anna's towering belligerence. They sat with her. They brought her their tokens. They ate her cake and drank her burnt coffee. They laughed about men, settled down to the subject of children. They offered her ancient gossip, tales of going and returning, stories of her own, truculent self. In this way they told her what to do. Anna listened, but she waited a day to come over. That way it looked like it was her idea.

Gram's front gate banged shut.

Then at the screen door, *Are you in there?* she said, seeing us both plainly.

Ma! Josie drawled, pretending, almost, that a battle hadn't raged for days. *Come in!* Josie turned to me, said in a low, purring voice,

Now pack.

Aunt Anna stepped in and surveyed the room. I was dusting while Josie stood ankle deep in magazines, deciding which were worth saving.

Ah God! This place is a mess! Who will take care of you? Aunt Anna could not quite speak to her daughter yet.

Ma, sit down. Take a load off. Josie was feeling triumphant, generous. *Mala will take care of us. She always does.*

I nodded to Aunt Anna.

And who will take care of you? she demanded of me.

I will, Josie said cheerfully.

Aunt Anna dropped to the couch and stared at us, Josie in her magazines, me in Gram's apron, a dust rag suspended in my hand, staring in surprise at Josie. She grunted and shook her head.

You'll have to take care of yourself, Mala. Dress warm. Eat a lot. The East is cold, wet and cold all the time. She was suddenly back on her feet. *I'd better help you both pack.*

I'm packed, Josie said quickly, then grinned at me. *But, I bet Mala could use some help.*

She was like a giant dust devil in Gram's tiny house, whirling through the rooms, ransacking the drawers. Every piece of warm clothing I had ever owned was laid out on the bed for me to fold, for her to refold. When she whirled off, I slipped those items too small or too hideous off the bed and kicked them under. In a moment of quiet, alone in Gram's bedroom, I retrieved the handkerchiefs. Then Anna was upon me.

What's that? she demanded.

Guiltily, I show her the handkerchiefs, a hundred delicate prayers.

I don't have to take them all, I told her. *Do you want some, Aunt Anna?*

She looked at me, askance, *What do I need those for?* She looked in my face. *You better keep them. You're the one going to the cold, wet East. You'll be sick all the time.*

In the other room, I heard her say to Josie, *Mala's taking all of Mama's handkerchiefs! Why is she taking all those handkerchiefs?*

Ma, I don't know. She loves those handkerchiefs. They laughed together, their first conversation in a long time. Holding the handkerchiefs to my chest, I listened and smiled.

Aunt Anna was now rooting in the kitchen. I showed her my choices for pots and pans.

Not that one, she grabbed a pot from my hand, shoved it back into the cupboard. *Too thin. Your sauce will stick.*

A tiny flame, like a gas burner, lit inside my chest. *My sauce never sticks.*

It will in that pan.

I wanted to protest, to tell her that I'd used that pan all summer, that it never stuck, but quite suddenly I had the vision of that pan, more than two thousand miles from Taylor, listening to Aunt Anna, obeying her firm command, sticking. Better not risk it. She picked a heavier pot, one I had heard Gram curse many times as she lugged it out, hauled it to the stove.

When Aunt Anna was done, Gram's house looked as if it had been struck by a biblical disaster. Everything Anna was making me take formed a great pyramid of boxes in the middle of the front room.

Come to dinner tonight, she ordered from the yard and marched away.

Josie eyed the pile in the front room, shook her head. *Two-thirds of that has got to go. Start sifting.* Sprawled across Eli's chair, she flipped through a discarded magazine. She was smiling.

You won, I commented shortly.

Josie lifted her eyebrows, *Of course.*

So, you're going to take care of me? I asked her dryly.

I've been taking care of you all along.

I made two visits before dinner, after my last Taylor dust storm had settled. Carrie watched me walk up the street toward the clinic. As I approached the picket fence she stood to meet me at the gate, blocking my passage.

I heard you're going.

Yah. We leave tomorrow early. Well, I amended. *You know Josie. Probably not that early.*

I'll be busy tomorrow, too.

I nodded. We both fingered the tips of the picket fence. The thick layers of paint were warm and malleable in the late afternoon sun.

I thought I'd be the one going, Carrie said finally.

I did, too. You still might, I added, knowing it was the wrong thing to say.

I don't want to, she stated, in her voice a thin edge of irritation.

I know, I told her, and reached out to touch the brown skin of her arm. She pulled away and stood, two feet back from the fence. Between us was the same secret we have shared all summer, but now I was on the other side of it. It was better to be the one leaving than the one left behind.

I gotta go make dinner, she said, and backed away toward the house.

I watched her go. Scrambled eggs with hotdogs, I thought and then prayed, *No, let it be something else, something wonderful. Pork roast, with roasted potatoes and carrots and lots and lots of garlic.* By the time I waved, she had disappeared.

Mrs. Miniverri answered my light knock in her apron. She, too, was preparing for dinner. The scent of lamb and rosemary filtered from behind her.

I wanted to say I'm sorry, I said through the screen door. *We're leaving tomorrow.*

She pulled me in and hugged me without a word. She left me among the green felt tables and rushed back to the kitchen. I heard the slight sound of spoon scraping pot, then a long silence. She returned with an envelope. I saw her name written across it in my own slanted handwriting. Feeling guilt like a heavy meal in my stomach, I opened the envelope. A recipe.

Cream soup, her voice so low in the pungent, still air. *Scallion and garlic. The trick is paprika, just a dash.*

I hugged her tightly, knowing it would not taste the same.

Do you want to see Johnny?

I hesitated, shook my head. Johnny and I had navigated The Sands together. He had led me to a place where we both heard the earth turning on its ancient, terrible wheel and heard, too the invisible forces that grasped and held life pinned to the dirt. We shared this. I wanted him to know. I wanted to tell him thank you for carrying me, but words were his enemy. The best I could give him was silence.

On the last morning, I cleaned Gram's house. I had already pared down my belongings to two boxes, one of household stuff and six Ball jars of Eli's wine, the other of clothes, shoes, winter coat, and one hundred handkerchiefs. Resting on top were three pictures, my mother in her wedding dress, and with my father by the black Cadillac. The third is of an old woman, white braids crowning an impatient scowl. From the cheap frame I could hear Gram insist, *Take picture! Take picture! Bread rise too much! Take damn picture!* The boxes sat by the back fender of Eli's car. So I dusted again, ran the sweep over the carpets, scrubbed the tub and sink, took newspaper and ammonia to the mirrors and window, listened for a change in Josie's breathing. At last she walked out of the back bedroom into the kitchen, arching her back, stretching, her mouth a wide, pink yawn.

Why are you cleaning? she asked, flopping into a kitchen chair. *We're gone. Who will care?*

I will, I told her and smacked a cup of coffee down in front of her. I did not tell her what I believed. Gram's ghost and all her memories would come back to her home once Josie's presence was gone. They would dance with dust motes and fill the kitchen with the warm smell of bread. Eli's chair would become once again inviolate. My father's mitt would again wander free. The house, the chair, the ghosts, they would wait with a settling patience for the next set of grandchildren to move in. It was the way the Wheel turned.

In front of Aunt Anna's house a small crowd gathered, the remaining family that had not preceded our departure with theirs, a few neighborhood ladies. Uncle Nick would return from his wanderings too late to say good-bye. I asked Aunt Anna to give him our love. She snorted and eyed our packed car suspiciously. It didn't look like enough stuff. Mimi and Kiki stood caged behind Aunt Anna's fence. Twin tears rolled down their faces. They waved white hankies.

Stop that blubbering! Anna demanded.

Mimi and Kiki blinked, clung to each other, awash in Anna's yard.

Uncle Milan stepped up, silently handed me a crumpled paper bag. Inside were the promised shoes. I pulled off my sandals and slid my dusty feet into the shoes. They were immediately comfortable, soft and sturdy.

I grinned at him and nodded. *They're perfect, Uncle Milan. Like those boots of yours. I could walk across the U.S. and Europe in these.*

He blushed, watched the shoes hungrily. How many times had he had the pleasure of watching someone put on his shoes for the first time? Aunt Anna elbowed him aside. She had Josie's accordion.

You almost forgot this! her voice shocked.

Ma...Ma! There's no room, Josie complained, but Aunt Anna was already wrestling the black and white accordion behind the passenger seat.

There's always room, Aunt Anna muttered, straining. The seat back gave an ominous pop. *There!* Aunt Anna said, satisfied, and stepped back, hands on hips. *Now you can practice at college!*

My seat angled forward, promising an uncomfortable ride. Josie laughed. Aunt Anna dashed back into the house as we finished our rounds of hugs and settled into the car. Aunt Anna came back out of the house and used her hip to bang through the front gate. She was carrying a vast chocolate-frosted sheet cake still in its pan. She slid it through the window.

For the road. Just keep it on your lap, she ordered me. It just fit in the narrow space between my chest and knees. Aunt Anna stepped back. She was blinking fiercely.

You get good grades! Both of you! And eat! She shook a finger at us.

Sure Ma... .

You'll be back! she warned us.

What for? Josie laughed, but the hard question was covered by the engine revving to life.

You'll be back! This is home! Aunt Anna called after us.

She waved desperately, stepping after us down the street. The small crowd watched her.

We took a victory lap through Taylor. Along Sixth Street old ladies in black stepped out onto porches, waved at us with floury hands. Men in undershirts thumbing garden hoses watched our passage. All through town, children had invaded cottonwood trees. They laughed from the branches and hung by knees or arms, bright, ripe fruit. School would start tomorrow. I noticed for the first time the cottonwood leaves, tinged with yellow. Summer was leaving, too. We drifted out of town, passed the road that led to the cemetery or the pool and out onto the northern plain that swept down from the eastern ridge of cliffs. We picked up speed. Ten miles out we passed the old Taylor ranch. A family by the name of Sandoval lived there now. They had installed a large, second-hand gas tank, rusted from some moister climate, and a gas pump. Over the low porch a sign hung hopefully: COLD DRINKS LAST CHANCE GAS. A forty-foot cowboy, brightly painted in red and blue with black boots, hat and gloves, was strapped with baling wire to the windmill next to the house. His jointed left arm raised, rigged to the mill. With the movement of the wind through the blades, he waved. Gram had loved this cowboy. Whenever we passed on a trip to visit her children in Salt Lake, coming or going, she greeted it with joy, laughing, waving back.

Hello, my friend, she'd call. *Look Mala, he welcome us... he tell us hurry home.*

Josie and I shot past. I stuck my head out the window, watched the cowboy beckoning to us through the screen of our dust. We arced with the road around a sweep of hills. Josie pulled over where the road crossed a gully. She came around the idling car, opened my door, pulled me and the cake out.

What's going on, Josie? I sputtered.

House cleaning, she said.

Releasing the passenger seat, she fought with the accordion, won the battle with a great noisy yank, and marched away with the sprung accordion limply sighing at her side. Still carrying the cake, I followed her up the hill. At the crest she hauled the accordion to her shoulder and flung it up and out over the edge. It flew, complaining, and landed far below with a prolonged, morose wail. She turned to me and took the sheet cake and threw it, too. As it sailed, pan fell away from cake, frosting lifted. Their flights continued along separate paths. The pan clanged against rocks, bounced, came to rest near the accordion.

You shouldn't waste food, Josie. And it was a perfectly good pan, I pointed out. *We could have used it!*

Josie just smiled, grabbed my hand, and ran with me back to the car.

Lightened, we raced east on Highway 50, the loneliest highway in America. We were emigrants like our grandmothers, leaving the land they created. Josie wanted to arrive in her new home empty-handed, clean, new. She peeled the layers of Taylor away from her, the people and the memories, until there was nothing left of that place but me sitting beside her. For her it was all dust.

As she discarded, I collected. A hundred stories, recipes, prayers, ghosts, delicate white handkerchiefs that I could unfurl and show to the wind that works to scatter them. I would still carry them when Taylor was gone. I carry them still.

I knew Josie was wrong. She would need them some day—the memories, the layers of home to wrap around her like a soft black sweater passed down by a grandmother, like a thick blue blanket to hide within when the world she created was too bright, too loud. I would be ready, ready with a loaf of fresh bread, perhaps a swig of sweet, homemade wine, and a government check. A story. I am the keeper of stories. I am family.

Acknowledgements

Though the towns of Taylor, Parker and their residents are fictional, all owe much to the stories my dad told as I grew up. Thank you, Dad, for sharing a place, time, and people who had such spirit, charm, and zest for life. There are hints of those stories here, though utterly changed. However, one tale is absolutely true. Dad did run away to box and win the Golden Gloves at the age of thirteen. Returning home, he earned a crack on the head with a frying pan for smashing the best-looking nose in the family. It was well worth it. Throughout the state of Nevada, that nose was legend, a badge of honor to his dying day.

Thank you also to my friends and readers, honest and patient to the last: Diana Kruse, Nelle Leifer, Carla MacMillan, Karen Zimba, Marcy Schwartzman, Marly Youmans, Hilda Wilcox, and Eve Pierson.

And to my dear friend Mary Marx who worked on every word of this story with me: Mary, like your pencil, your insights are sharp and true, and like your nook in the library, your heart is always open and welcoming. Thank you.